AF349001

OBJECTS ARE PEOPLE TOO

OBJECTS ARE PEOPLE TOO

Justin Sutcliffe

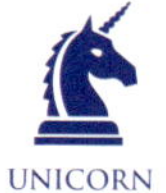

UNICORN

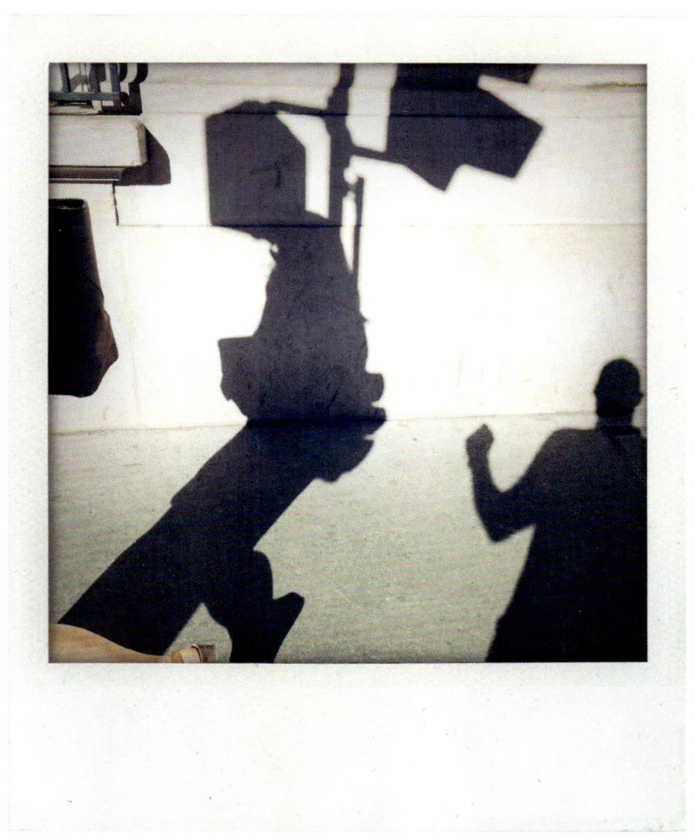

The Author – Paris

INTRODUCTION

JUSTIN SUTCLIFFE

THEY APPEAR TO ME anywhere and everywhere. In the mundane and the extraordinary, while I'm making a completely different photograph or when I'm least prepared. Some people look for them but I actively try not to.

When I first started to notice these imagined faces, it was very occasionally and I enjoyed it with wry humour. But very soon they seemed to be everywhere, which was an intrusion and problematic for my work as a professional photographer. So I began consciously refusing to see them.

For the most part, this solved the issue and the world went back to being itself. A walk in a city or the countryside was just that, no longer a parade of expressions around me or beneath my feet at every step. Occasionally, despite my efforts, a face might appear. So instead of banishing it from my mind, I would accept it and make a photograph with the Polaroid camera I carried almost constantly. Anything that made it through the barricades had sort of 'earned its place' in my consciousness. These pictures felt personal and were mercifully infrequent.

As Polaroid film became scarce, I turned to another solution, my iPhone, with an app that simulated the colour palette and the distinctive stippled border of the iconic 600 film.

A handful of photos became quite a few, and suddenly, there was the beginnings of a project. At that point, I decided to give myself some structure.

First, I never *tried* to see the faces. I had a big enough challenge trying to *prevent* almost any group of circles and lines from subconsciously reorganising themselves into expressions, so the idea of looking for them was absurd.

Secondly, no rearranging or staging. I would occasionally try to look at the face from a different angle to 'find its best side' but I didn't tidy it up or try to improve it. I wanted to make something personal, not perfect.

A recurring phrase became my guiding principle: 'nothing sought, nothing staged'.

As time went on and the project took shape, a third boundary developed, nothing obvious. Most of my photographs stem from the random (sometimes momentary) coincidence of objects that are not necessarily related. Perhaps my decision to try avoiding seeing too many meant that the very straightforward type of 'drunk octopus wants to fight' memes just never really appeared or appealed.

On the face of it, making a body of work on the principle of avoiding your subject seems a bit contrary; completely the opposite of what one would usually do. The result has been something organic and unhurried, which might be part of what appeals. All my other photographs are consciously made and nearly always with some kind of time limit. This series was free of all structure because its very nature was unintentional.

What became apparent when looking at the dates on my phone was how the photos came in clusters. There might not be any for months and then suddenly a flurry, like proverbial buses – nothing for ages, then half a dozen all at once. Looking through these pictures in the context of other photos from that day or week, showed patterns emerging – faces appeared more often when I was in very heightened emotional states; periods of intense happiness or pressure or focused concentration. At one point, while moving house, the presence of faces was so constant that I wondered if I'd lost my ability to tune them out.

During most of the two decades covered in this book, I was working as a photojournalist, frequently overseas and often in confrontational places. So there are moments from Afghanistan and Libya alongside the everyday life of making breakfast or getting groceries. My slightly obsessional practice of suddenly producing my phone and taking aim at seemingly random or irrelevant things often drew funny looks from passers-by and friends.

On one particularly difficult day in Misrata, Libya, I was on assignment with my colleague Christina Lamb and we visited a locally infamous internment camp for arrested refugees. The conditions there were shocking and access was granted somewhat reluctantly. Our hosts viewed us suspiciously as we toured the cramped and squalid detention centre. At one point I was suddenly taken by a face that appeared from two discarded coffee cups the guards had littered in some half-built concrete blockwork. Without thinking, I switched to my phone to make the photo. A tense silence suddenly descended, the guard looked sternly at me and spoke with our interpreter who asked me what I was doing. Even as I explained to him, it seemed objectively odd. Watching as he translated my explanation into Arabic seemed to make it even more ridiculous. Neither men could comprehend why I was switching my attention in this way. The change from professional camera to phone had looked highly suspicious. I should have known better. I *did* know better! I resolved to be more mindful and never repeat the mistake.

Most of my pictures were far more light-hearted by comparison, and I would sometimes laugh out loud as I was taking a photo – which might have seemed somewhat unhinged. When one of our two rescue cats left the outline of a face in her dried food, I couldn't help feeling that she'd done it on purpose.

'Oh, you've got to be kidding me!' became a frequent expression to myself as a face unexpectedly appearing in some objects that I saw nearly every day and had never noticed before. Then, just as surprisingly, it would never appear to me again.

The choice of title – *Objects Are People Too* – was born out of a sense that in a world which perpetually objectifies people, I might be somehow personifying objects in a strange convergence.

This is a deeply personal journey, filled with expressive imaginary 'people'. It's a long-running moment of levity set against the backdrop of a life often faced with recording the most serious aspects of human existence. And even the challenging moments have given rise to pictures that make me smile and laugh. I hope you'll feel the same as you turn the pages.

Justin

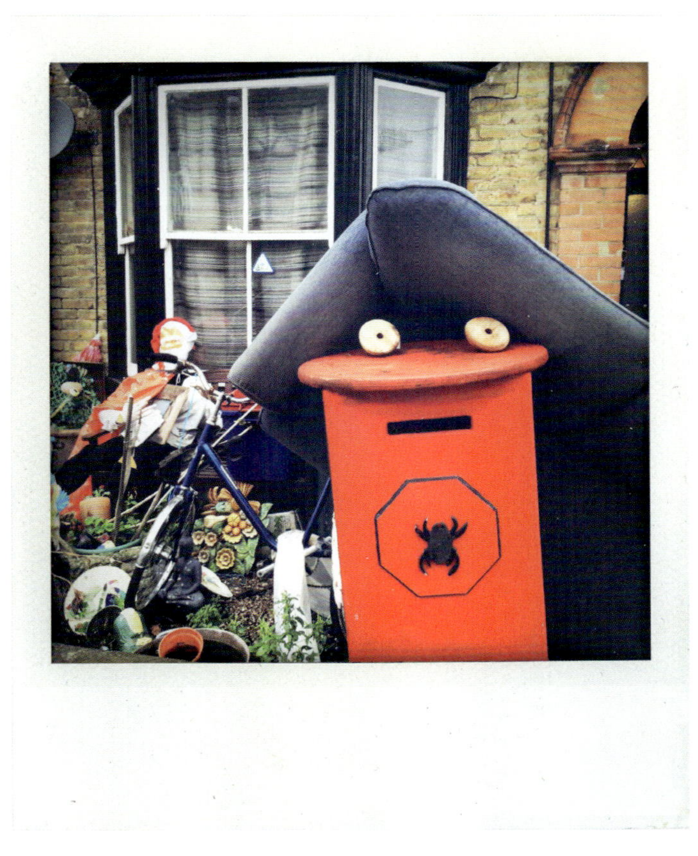

Front garden – Whitstable, Kent

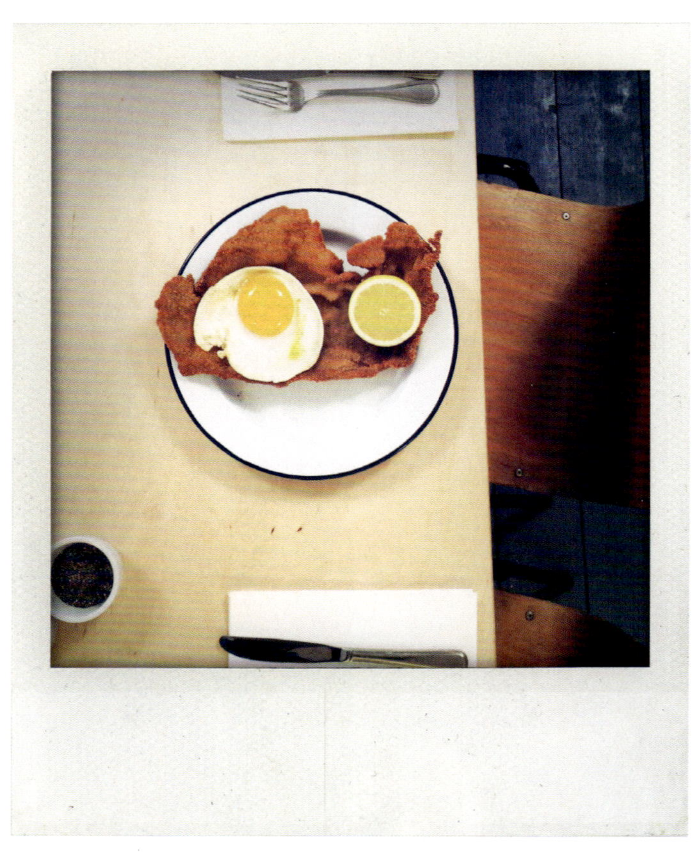

Schnitzel – Boopshi's, London

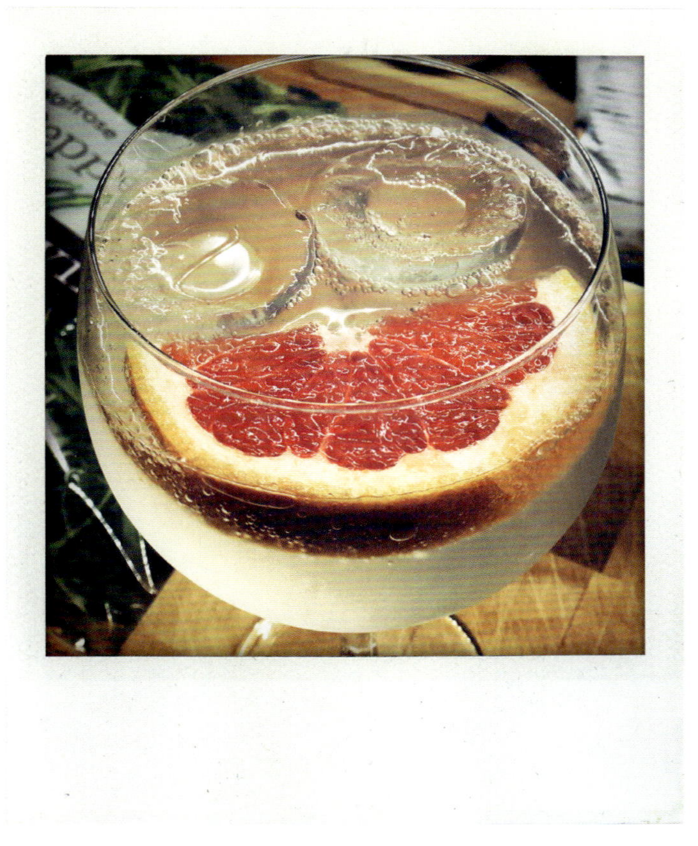

At home

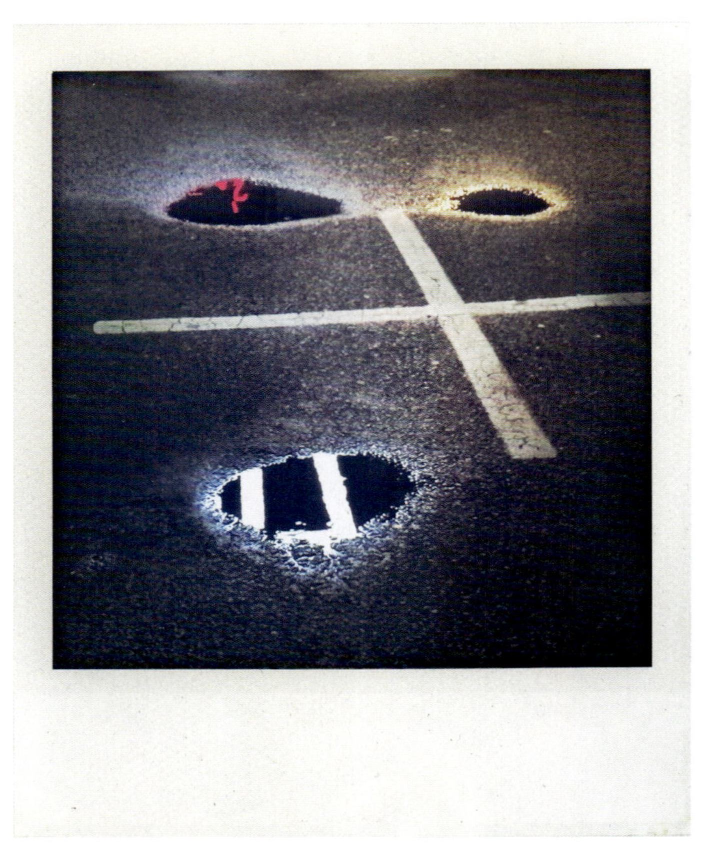

Car park – Ipswich, Suffolk

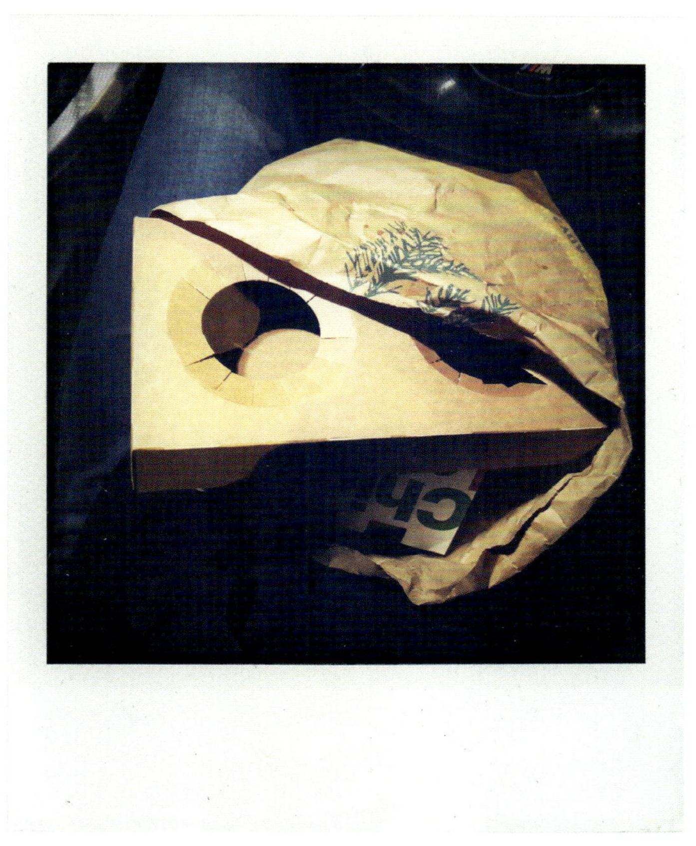

Takeaway cartons

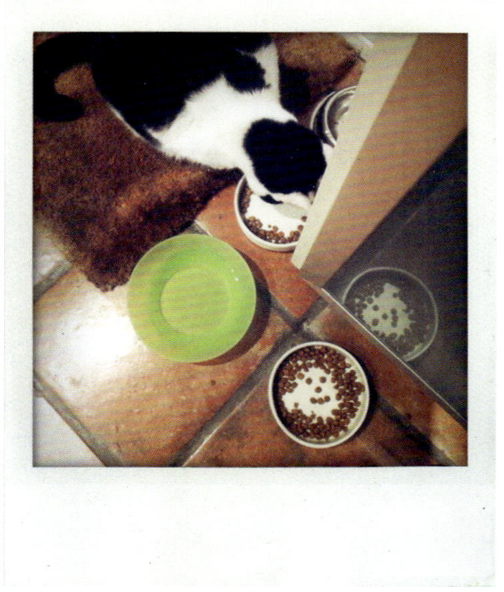

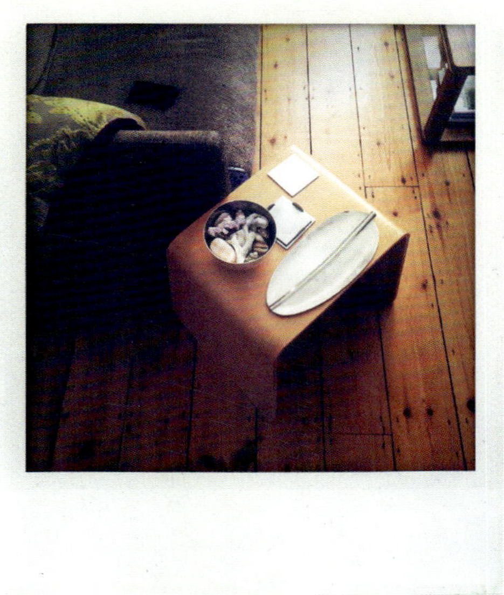

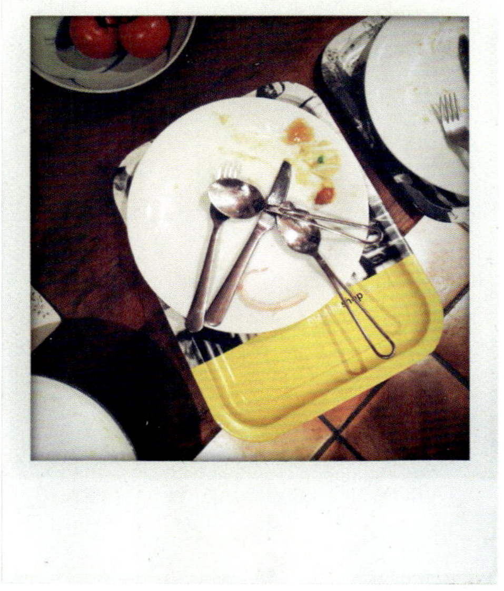

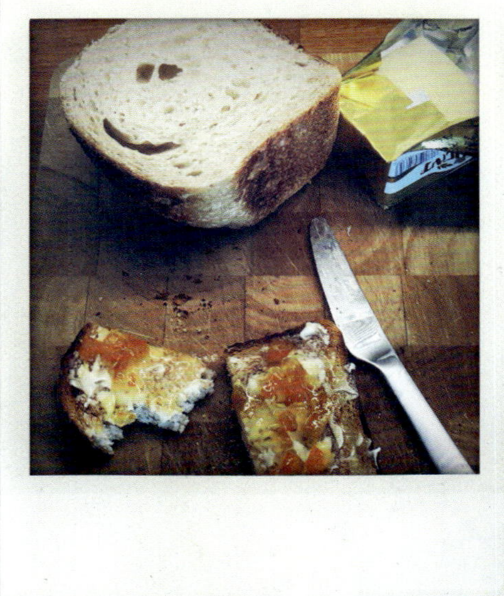

Cats' bowls – Home
Clearing up after lunch

Ornaments and table
Making breakfast

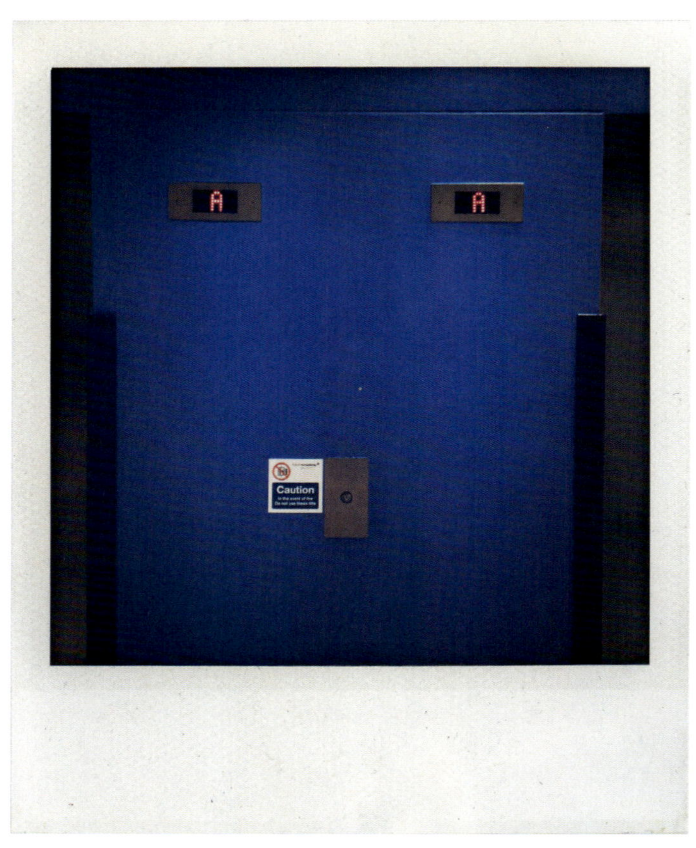

Lifts in an apartment block – Docklands, London

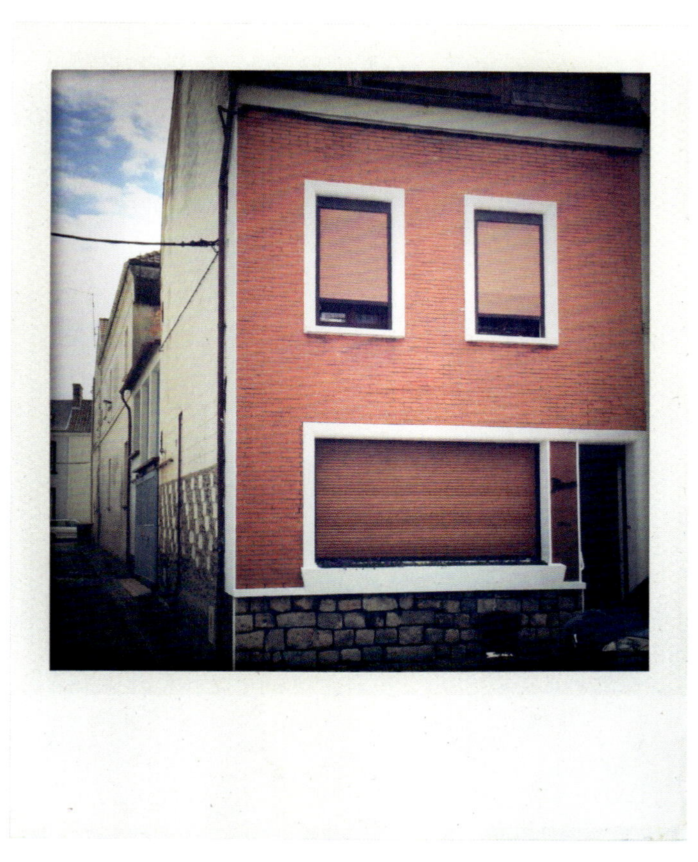

Sleepy house – near Montreuil, France

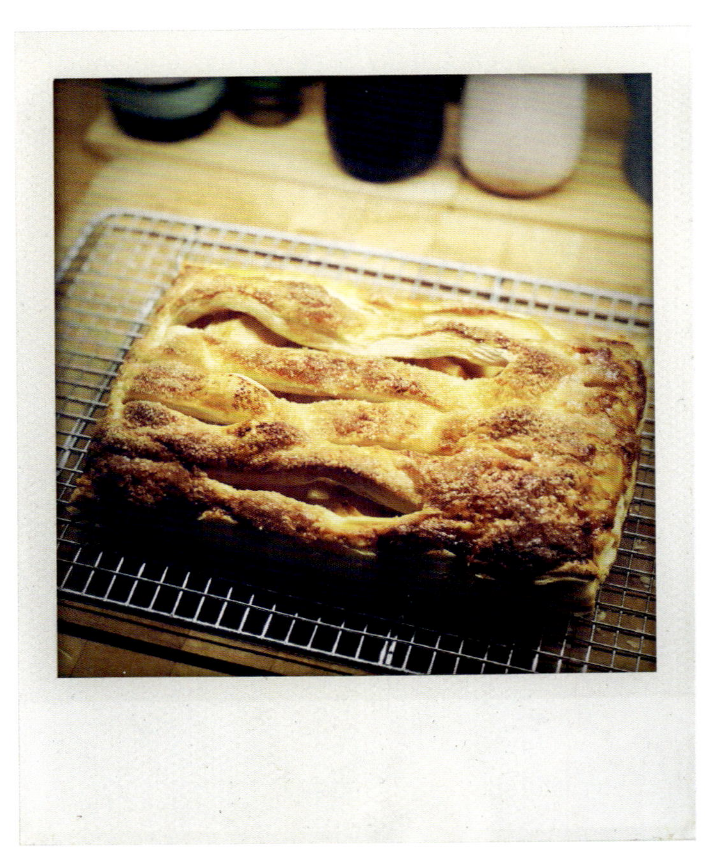

Homemade apple pastry

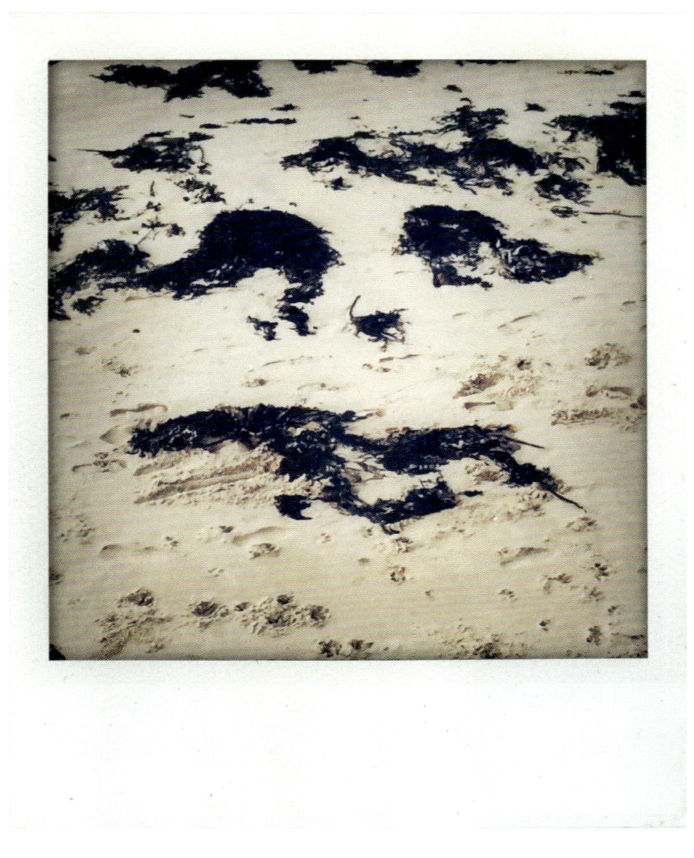

Beach after a storm – Margate, Kent

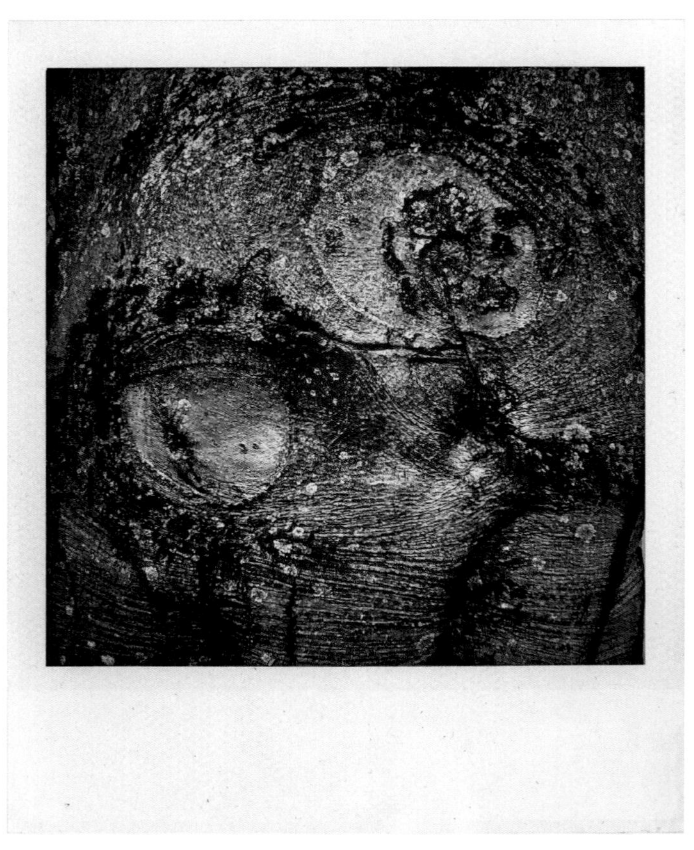

Cat-face tree – Blean Woods, Kent

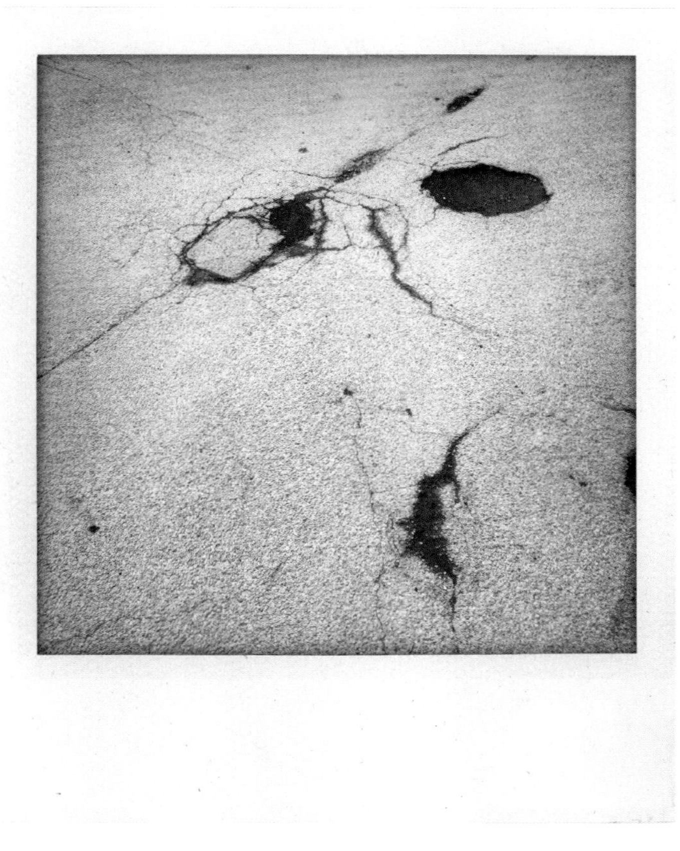

Pavement – Folkestone, Kent

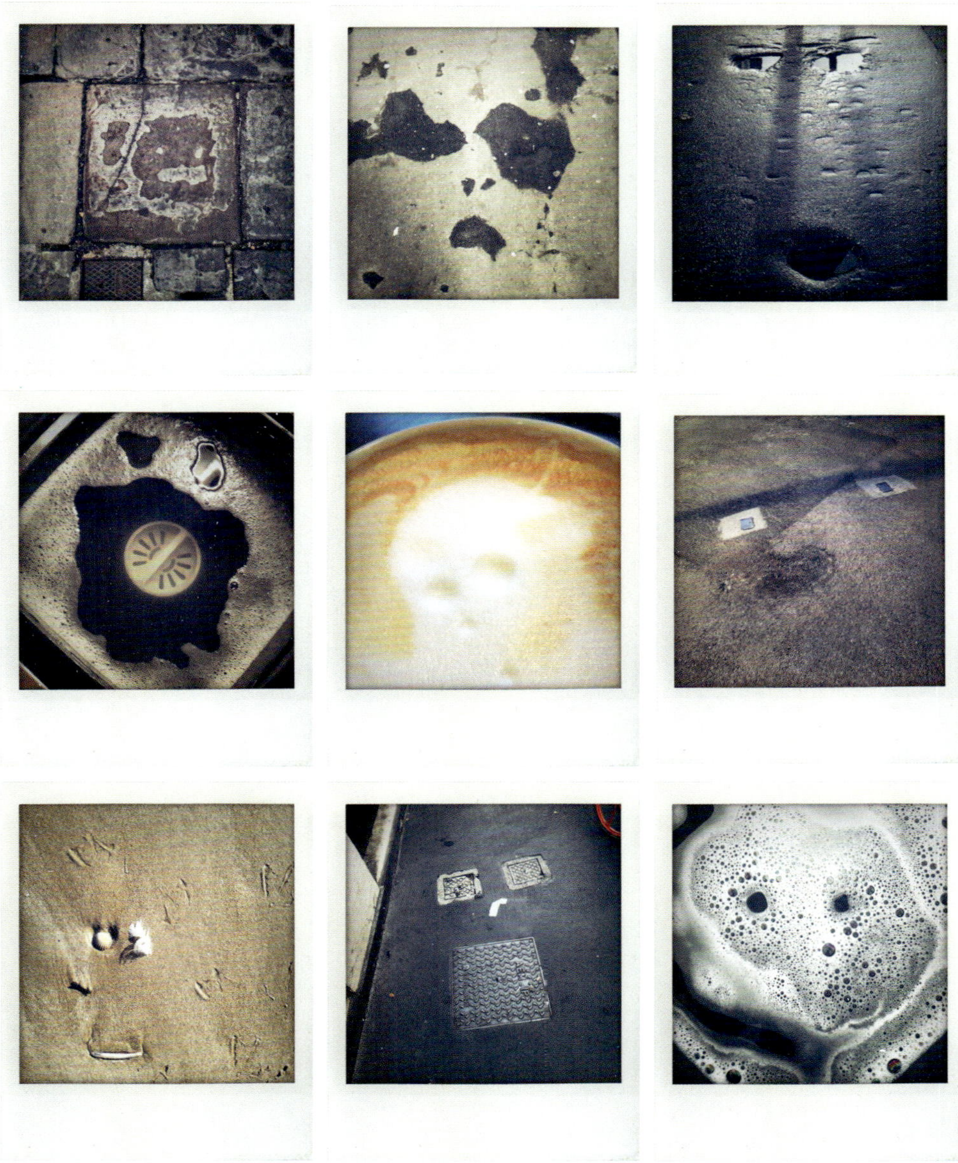

Frome, Somerset
Washing-up bowl
Camber Sands, East Sussex

Car park – City of London
Coffee skull – London
Pavement – Milan

Sidewalk – Paris
Pavement – Lancaster
Washing-up bowl

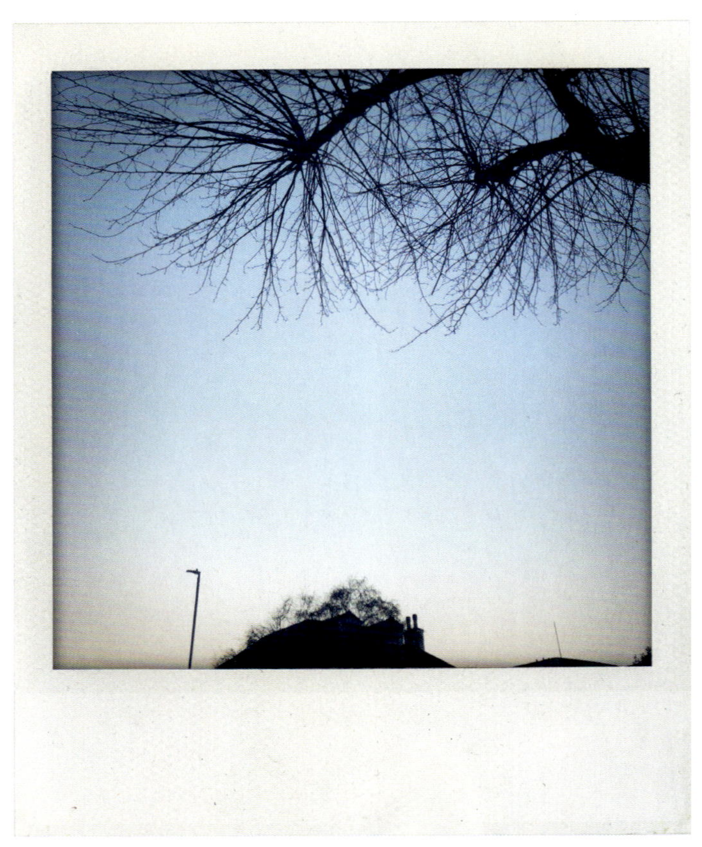

Dusk – Folkestone, Kent

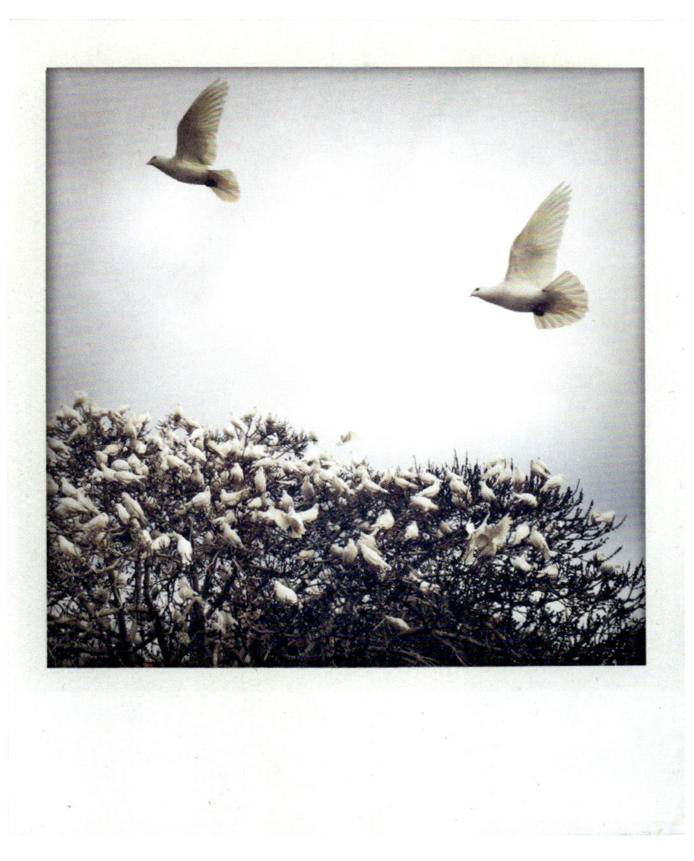

Doves – Mazar-i-Sharif, Afghanistan

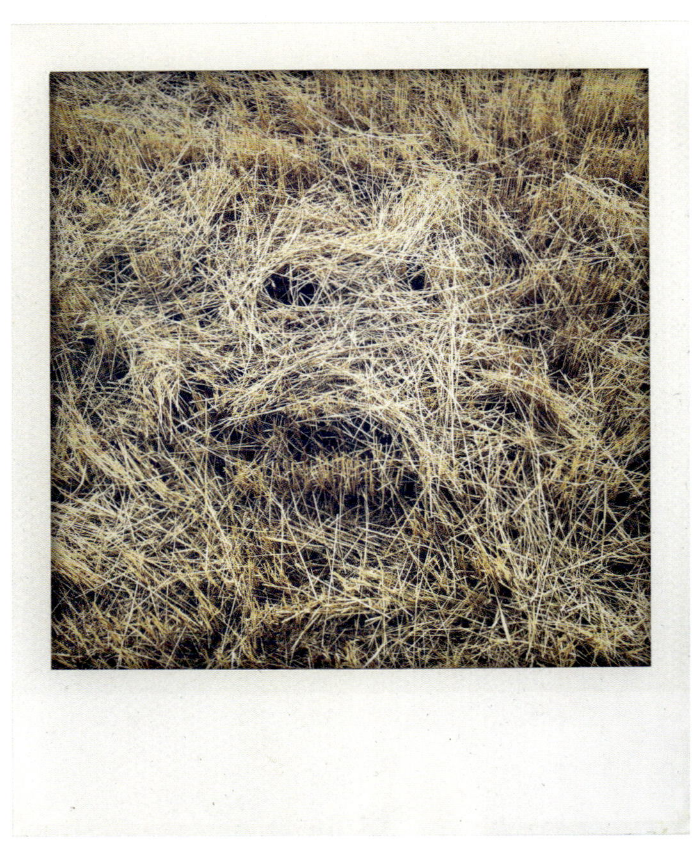

Hayfield – South Downs, East Sussex

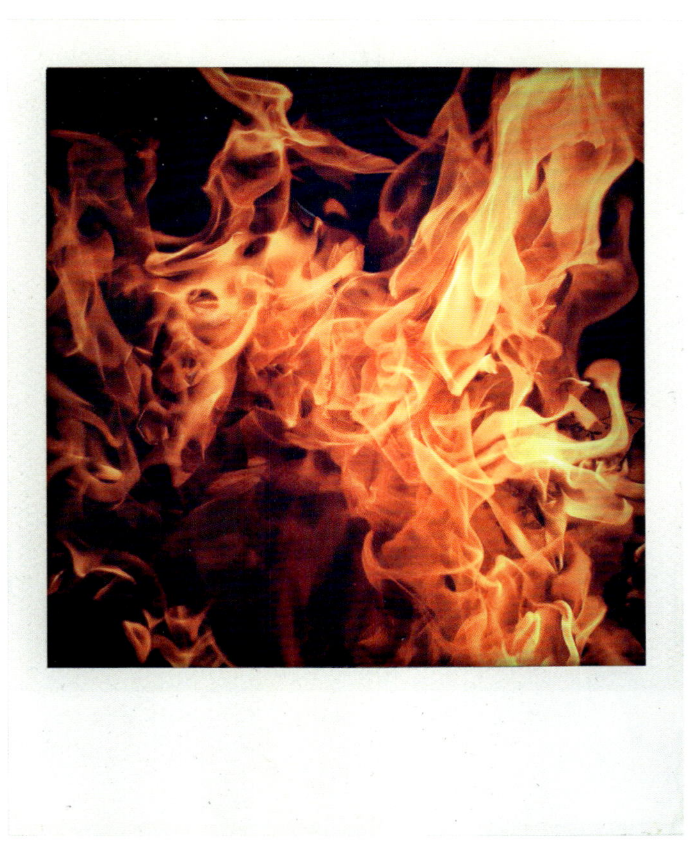

Brazier – Whitstable, Kent

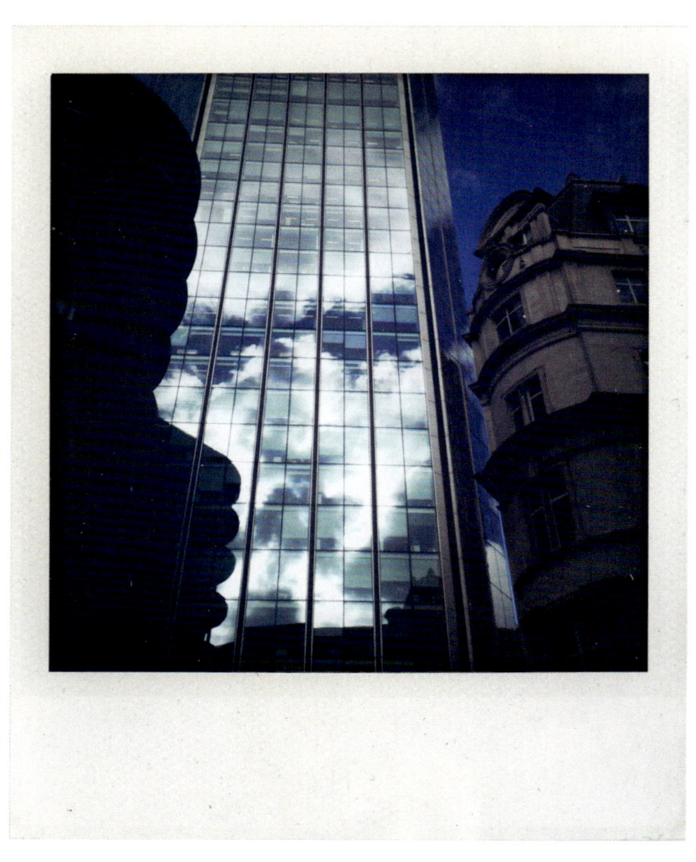

Reflected face in the clouds – City of London

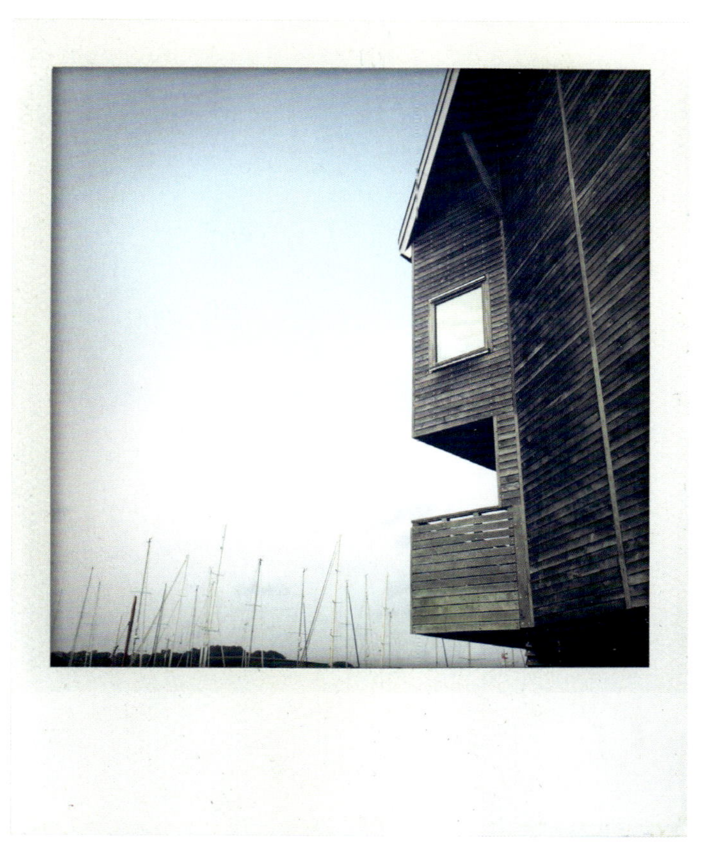

Marina – Falmouth, Cornwall

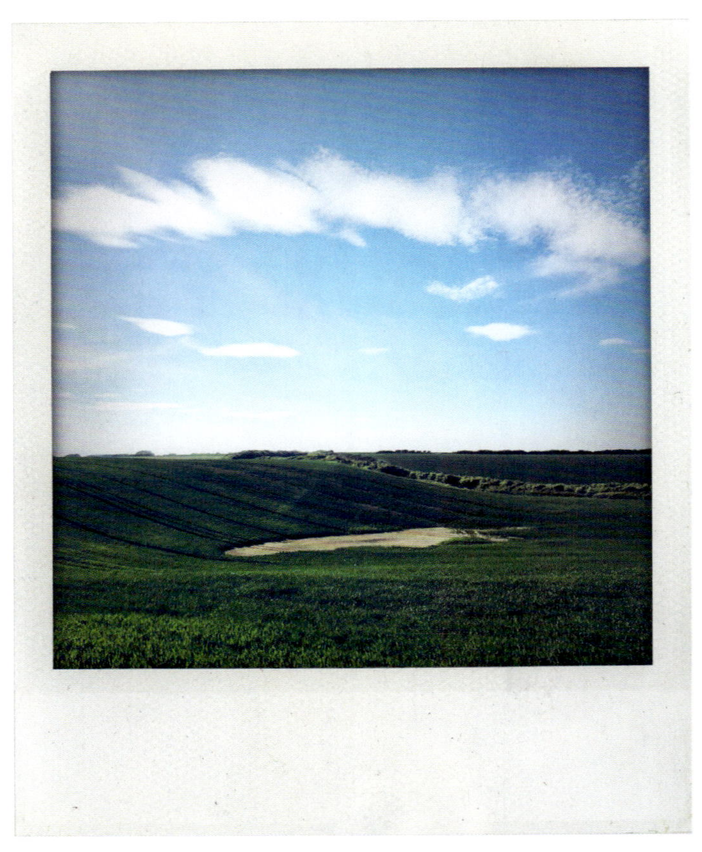

Near Capel-le-Ferne, Kent

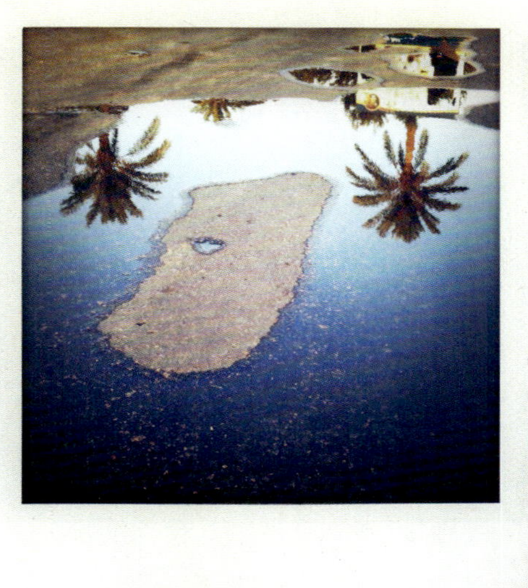

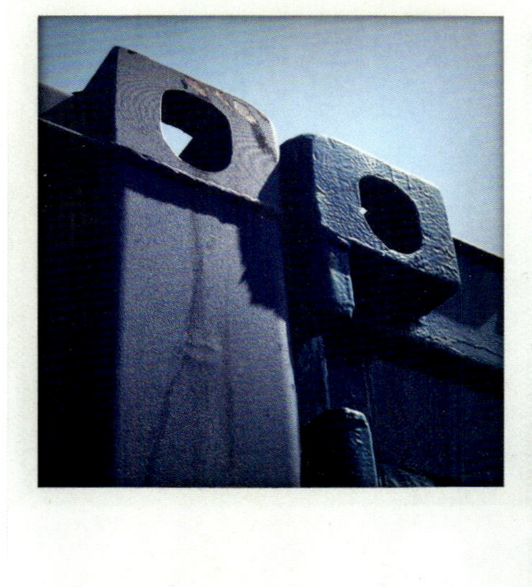

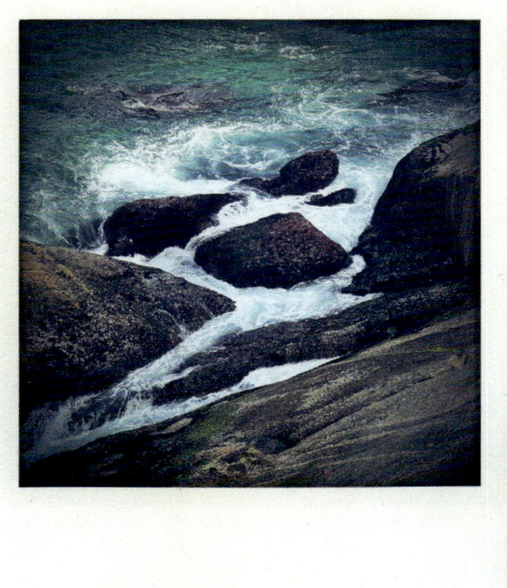

Folkestone, Kent
Shipping container – Folkestone, Kent

Misrata, Libya
Rocks – near Leblon, Rio de Janeiro, Brazil

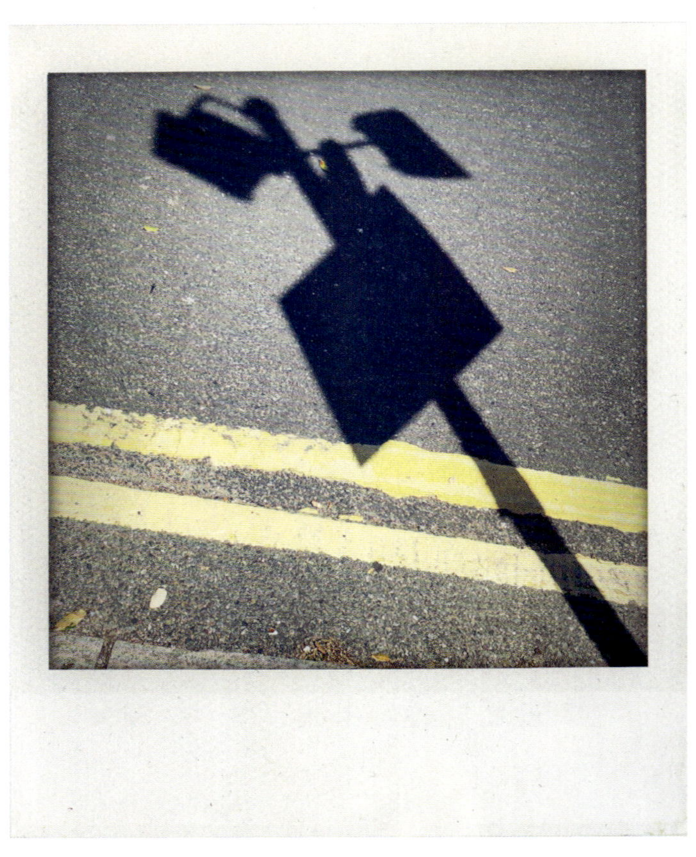

Double yellow lines – Brighton, East Sussex

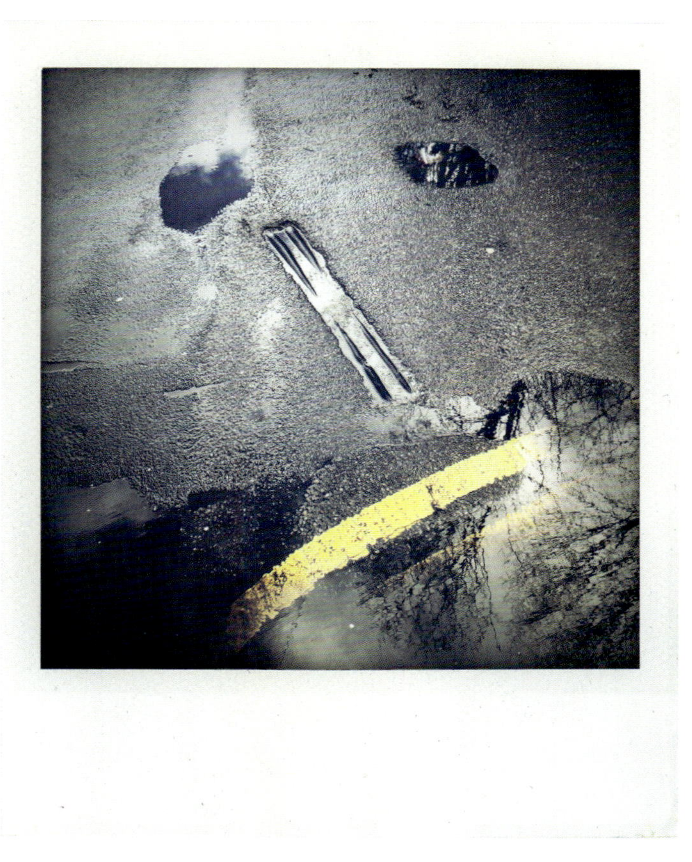

Double yellow lines and reflection – Loncon

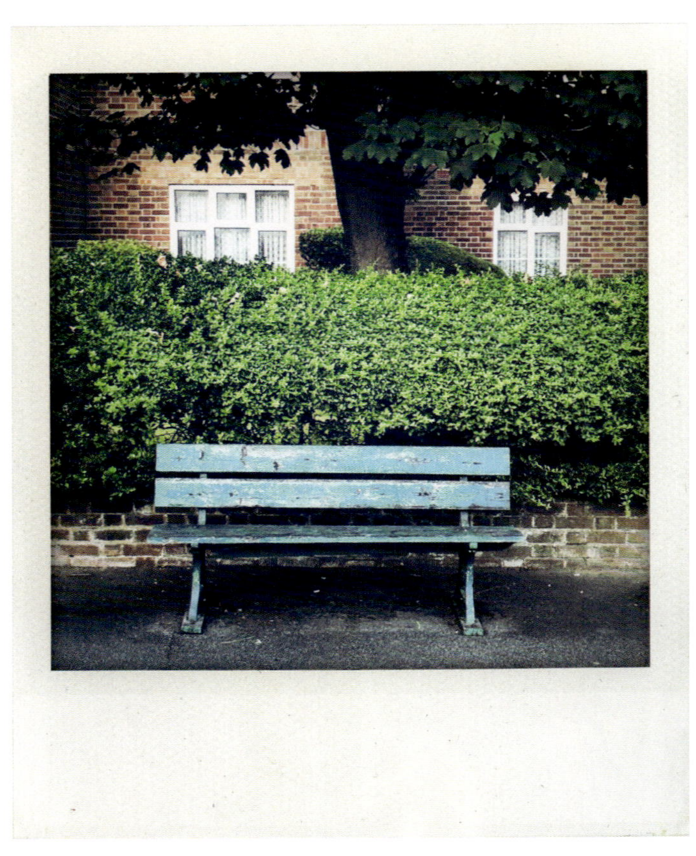

Street bench – Folkestone, Kent

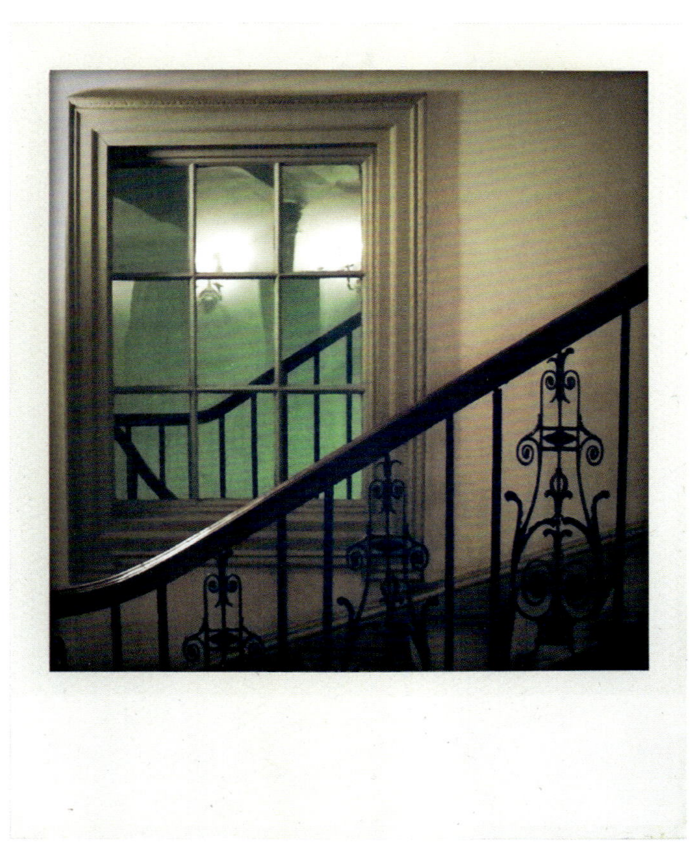

Somerset House staircase – London

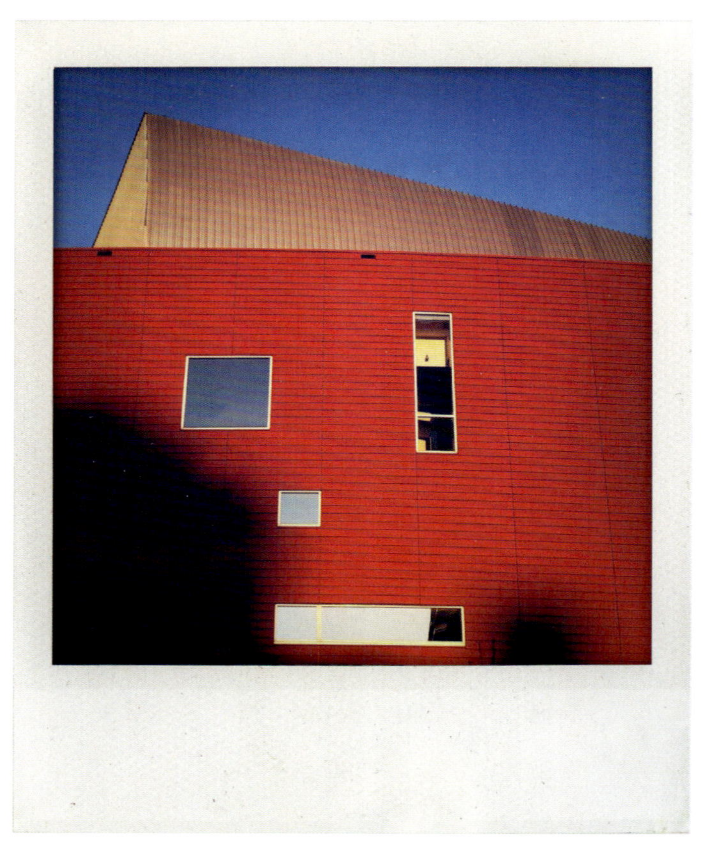

Rotterdam, Netherlands

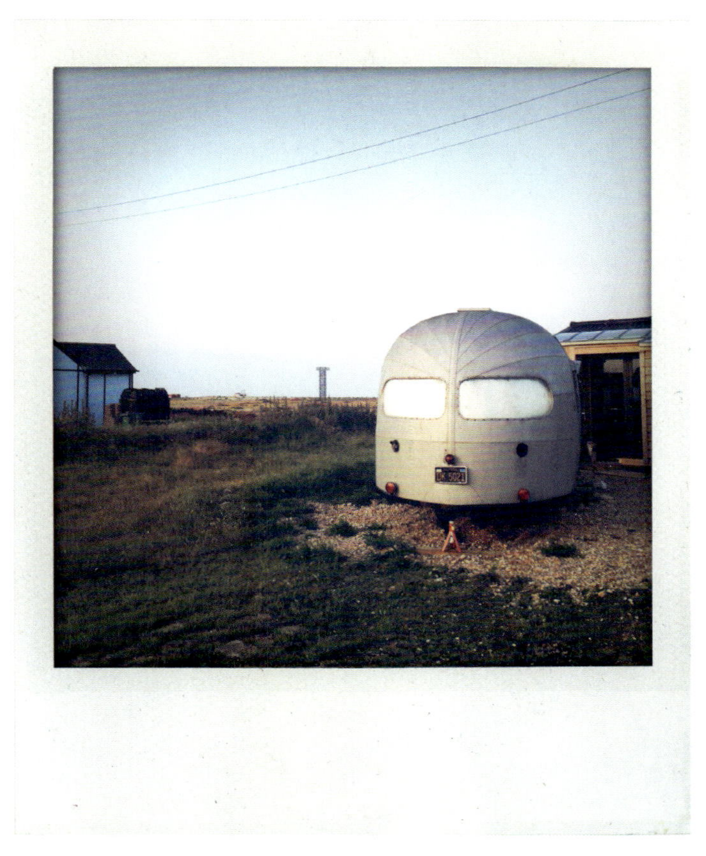

Dungeness, Kent

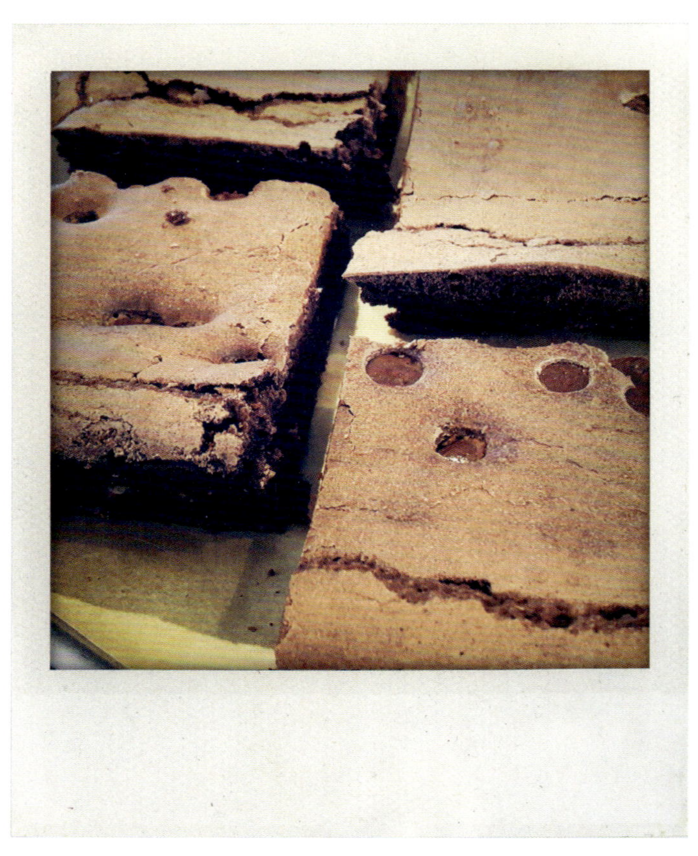

Brownies – Harbour Coffee Co., Folkestone, Kent

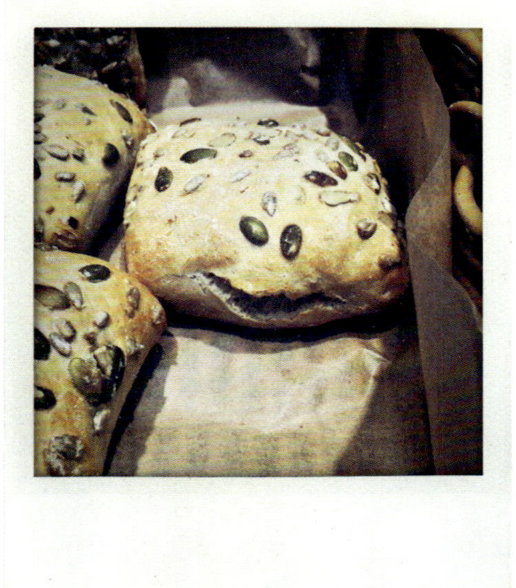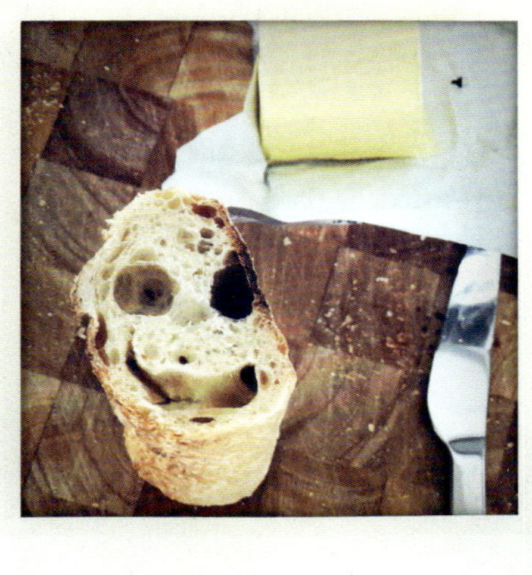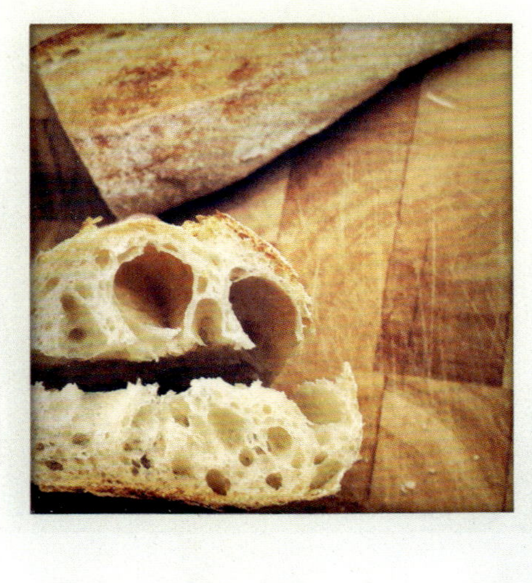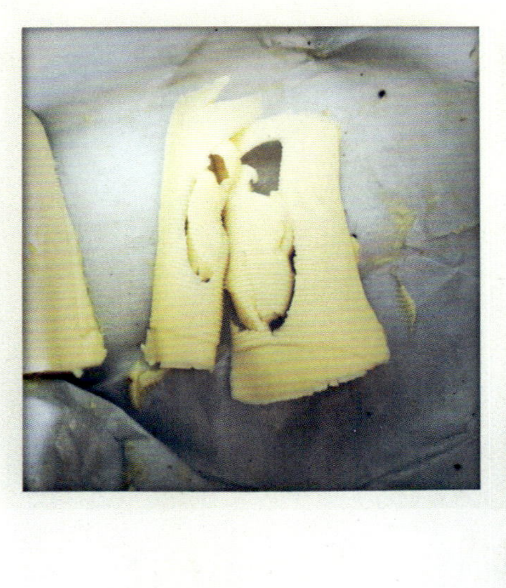

Bread roll – Whitstable, Kent
Breakfast – Home

Breakfast – Home
Breakfast – Home

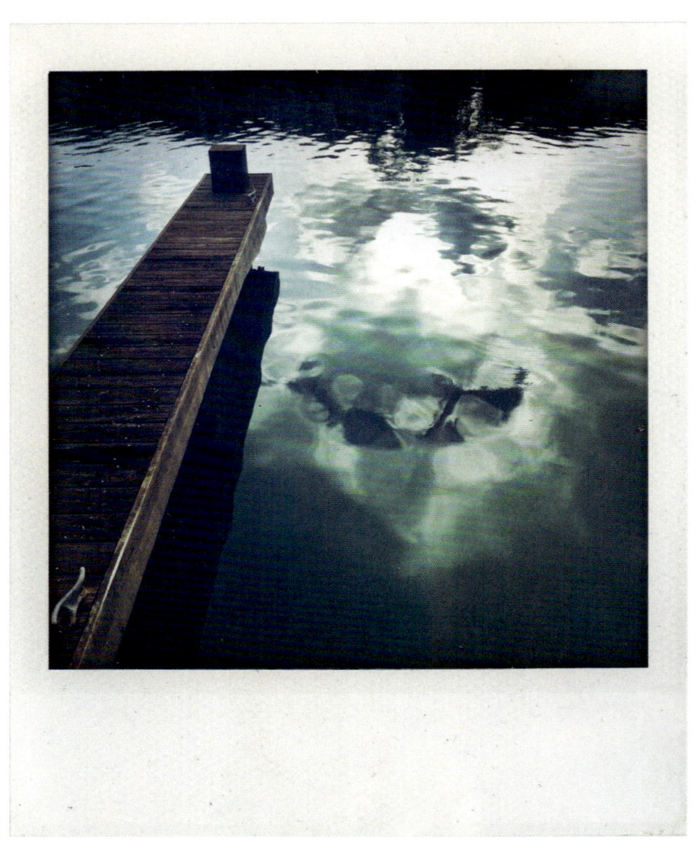

After the hurricane – English Harbour, Antigua

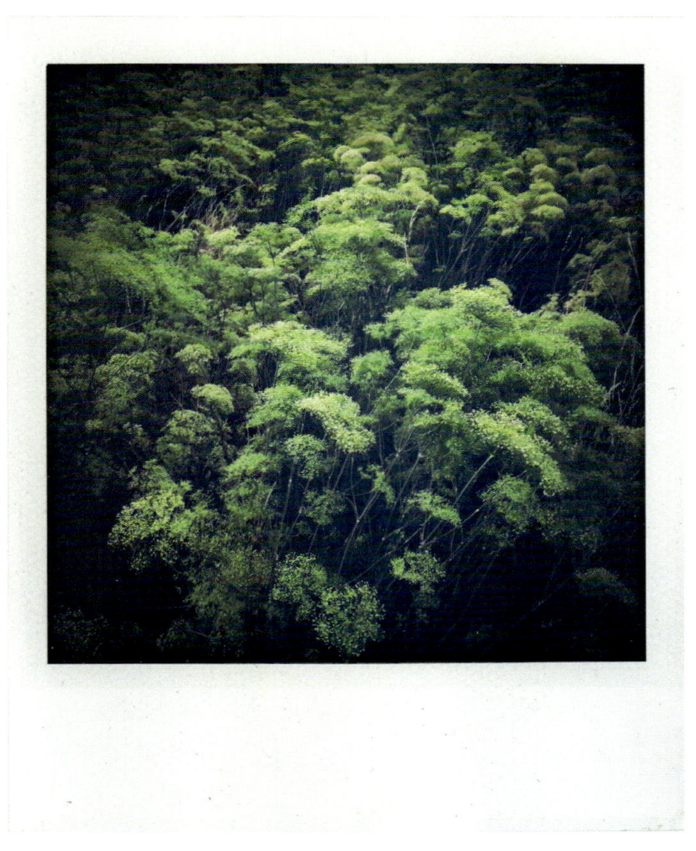

Tankerton, Kent

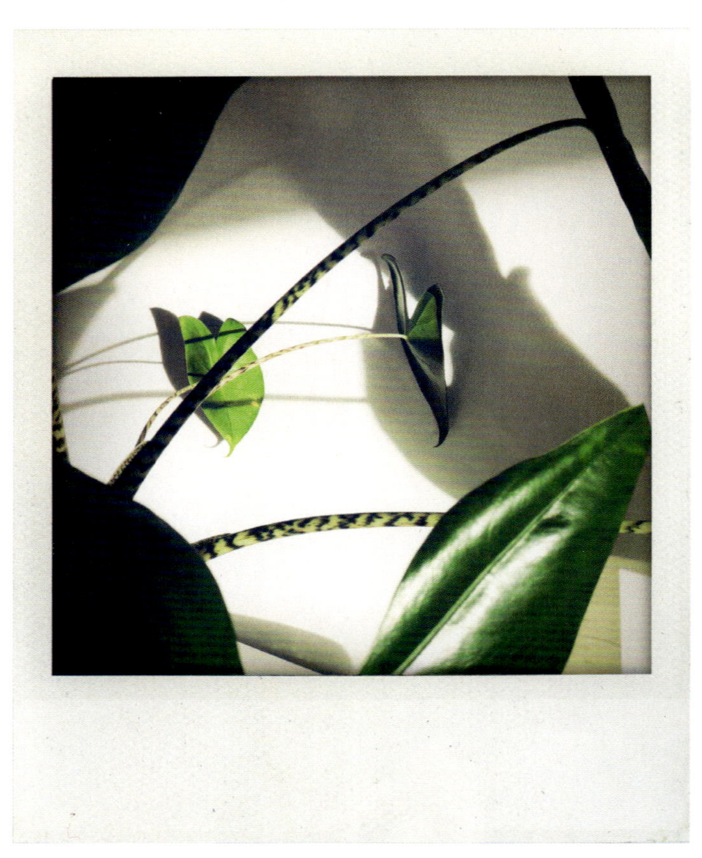

Zebrina – Home

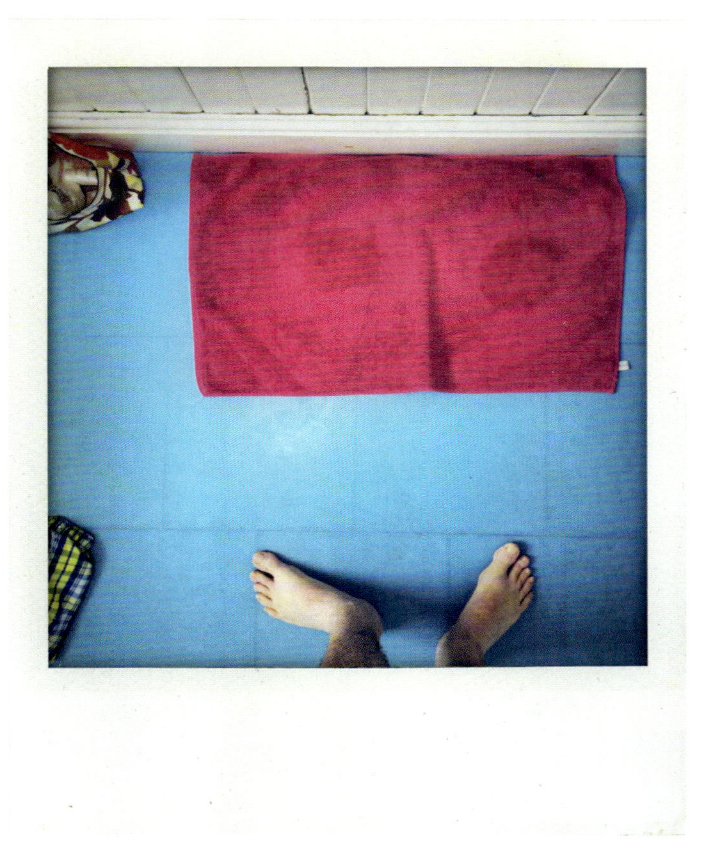

My feet – Home

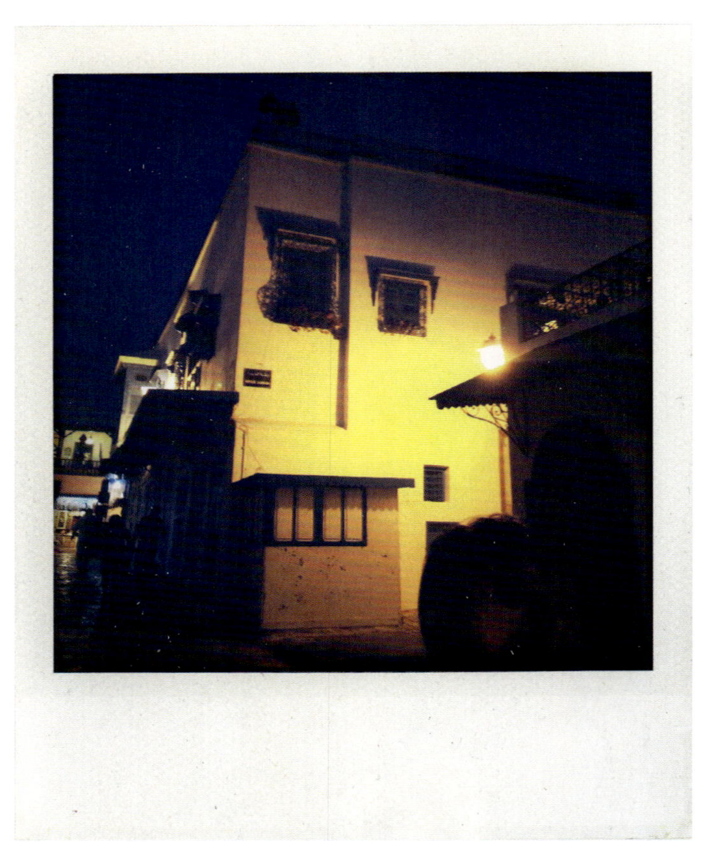

Back street – Tunis, Tunisia

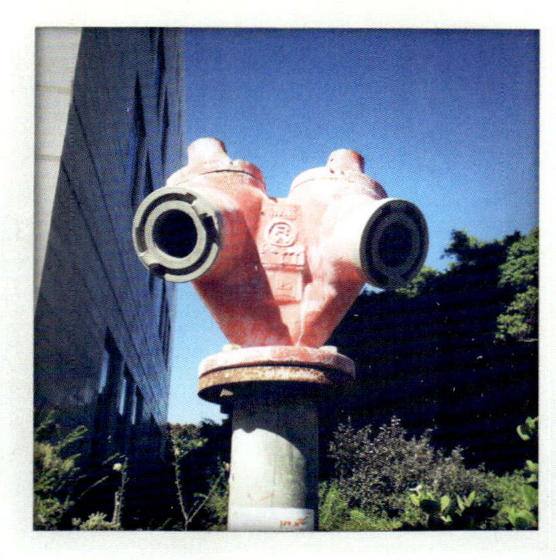

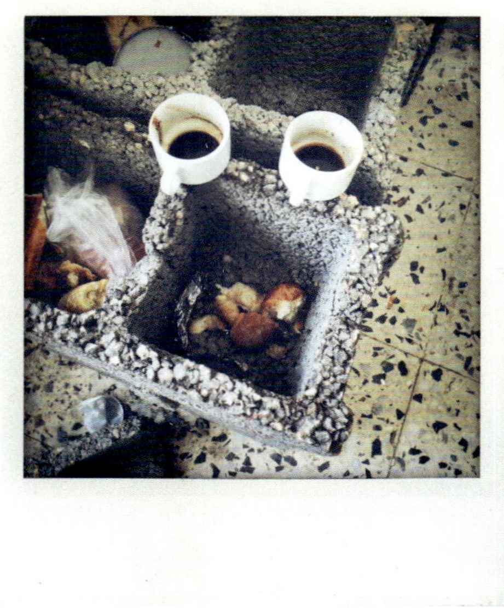

Fire hydrant – Tel Aviv, Israel
Internment camp – Misrata, Libya

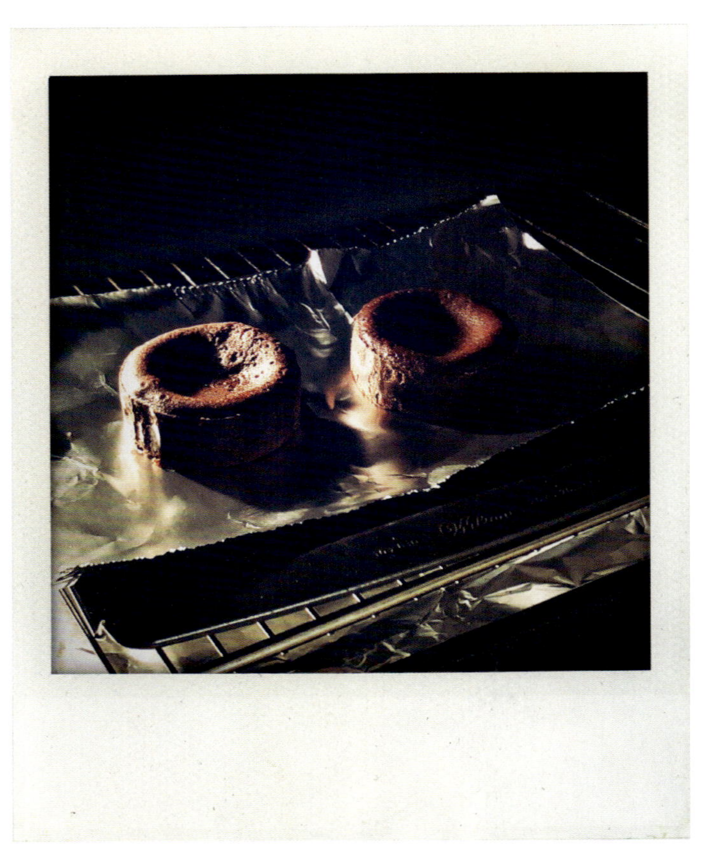

Puddings – Home

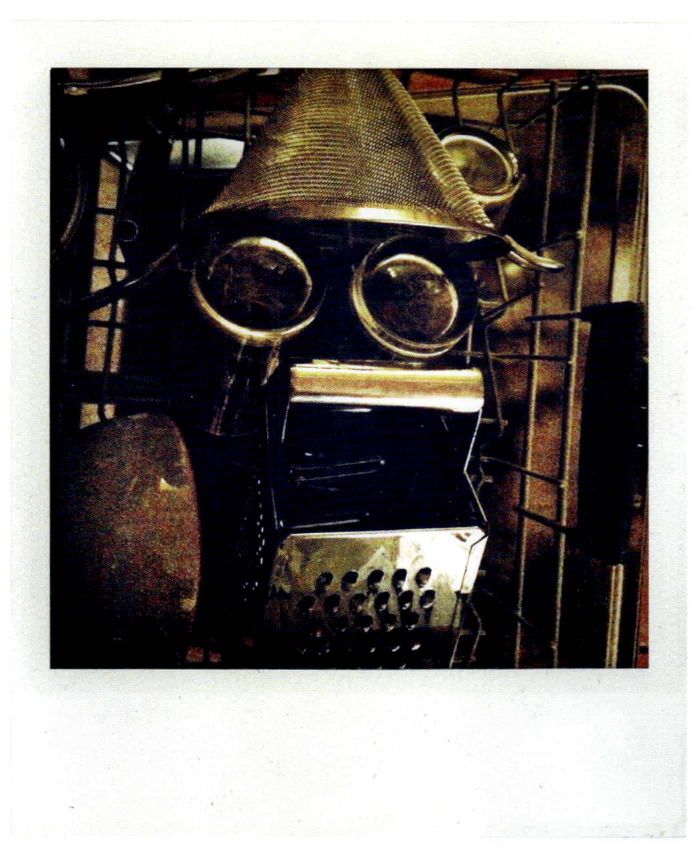

Random dishwasher face – Home

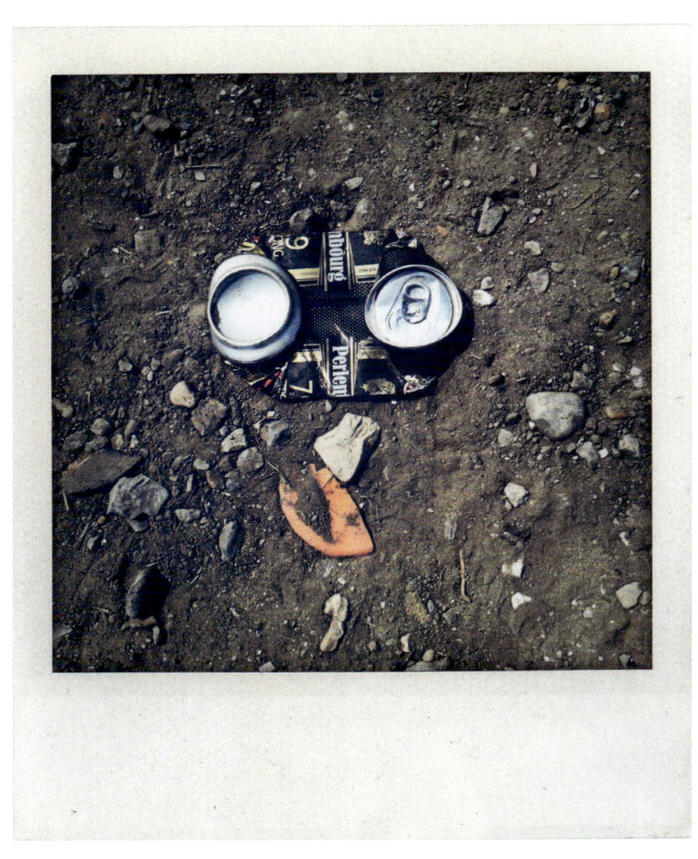

Crushed beer can – Eritrean section, Calais camp

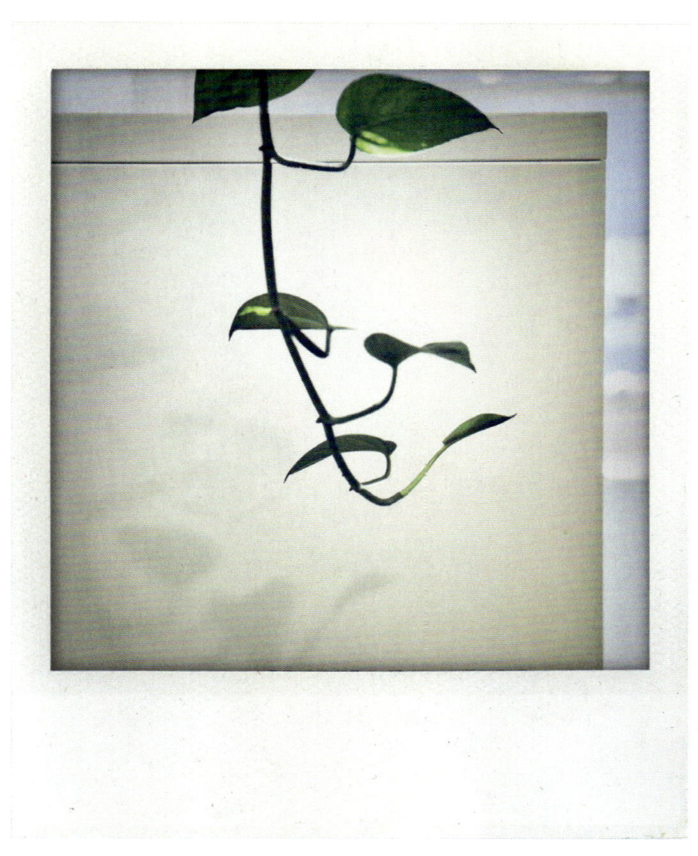

Office plant and filing cabinet – Folkestone, Kent

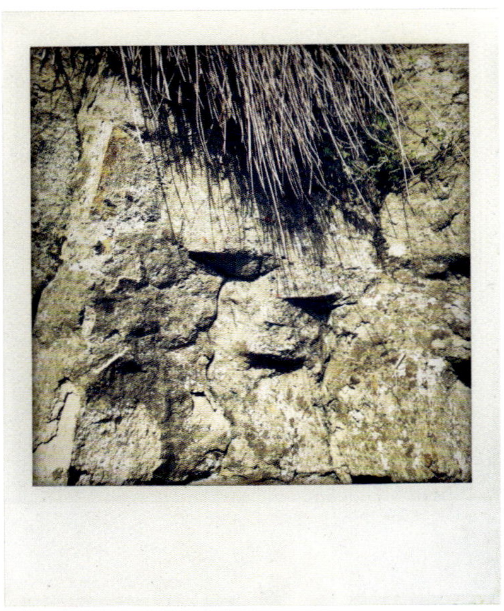

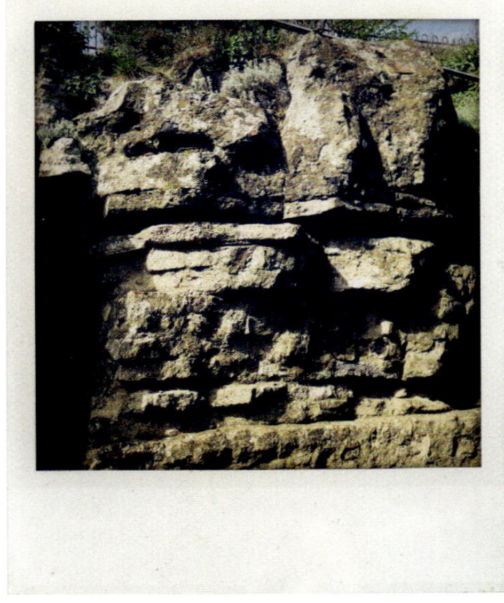

Rock faces – Folkestone, Kent

[52]

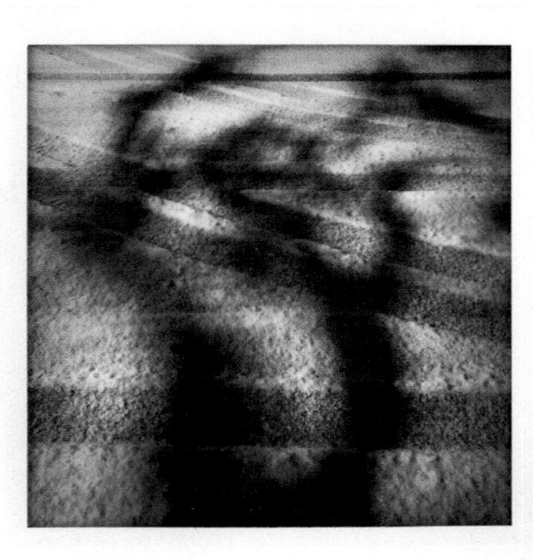

Creepy snow figures – Folkestone, Kent

Setting sun through the top window – Home

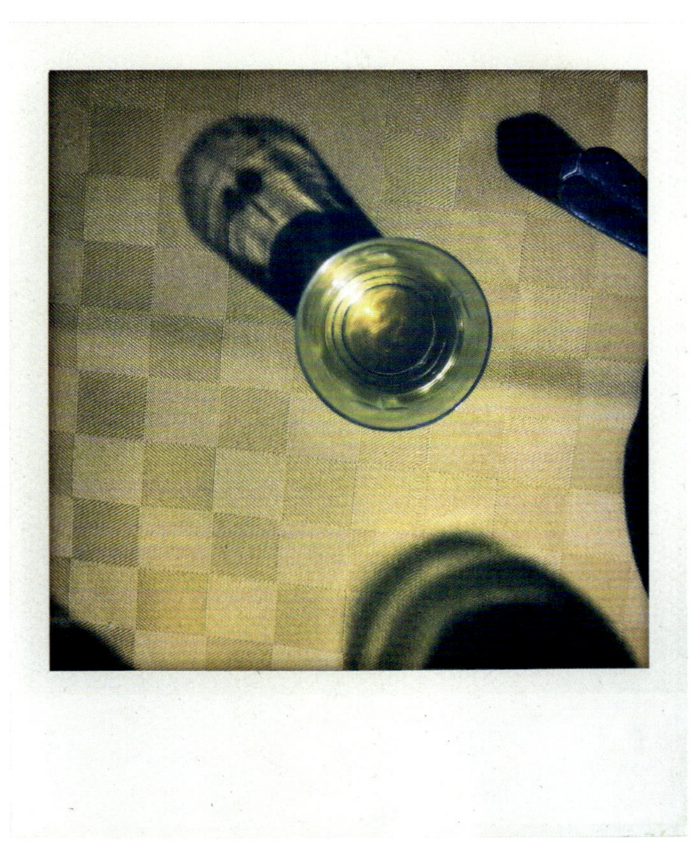

Before food arrives – Village in the Valtel.ina region, Italy

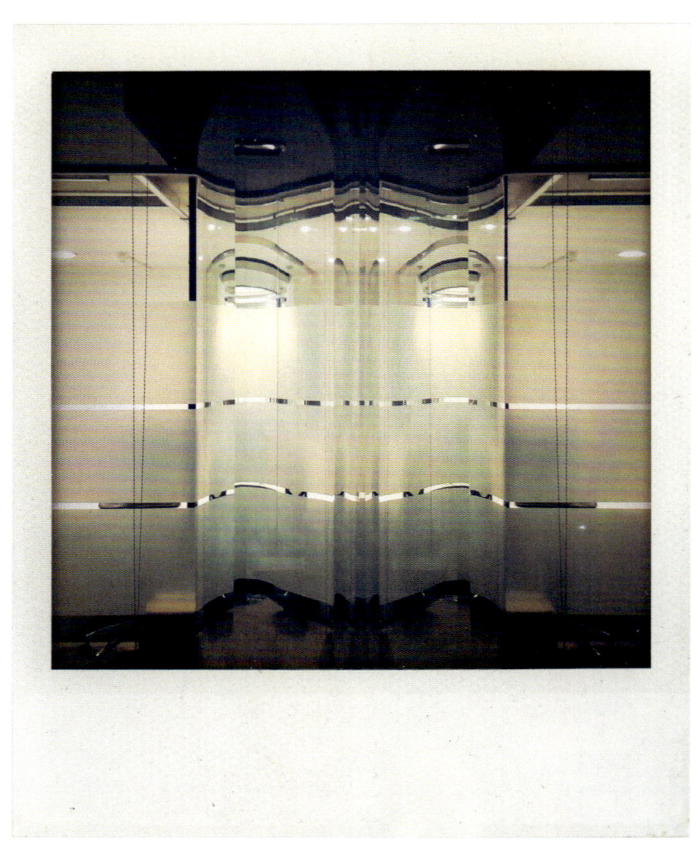

Hotel conference room – Kent

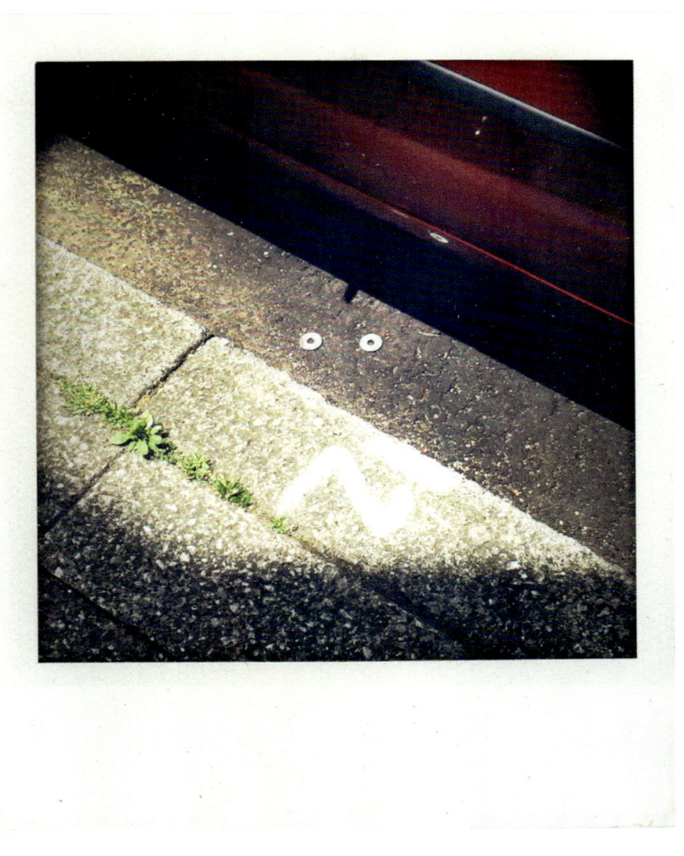

Pavement – Whitstable, Kent

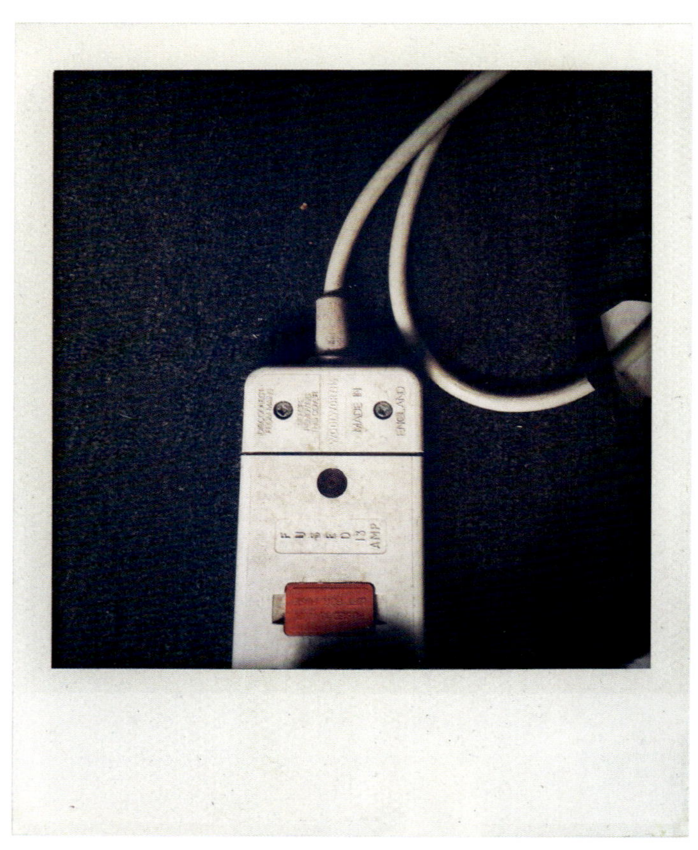

Susan Glenn's plug – London

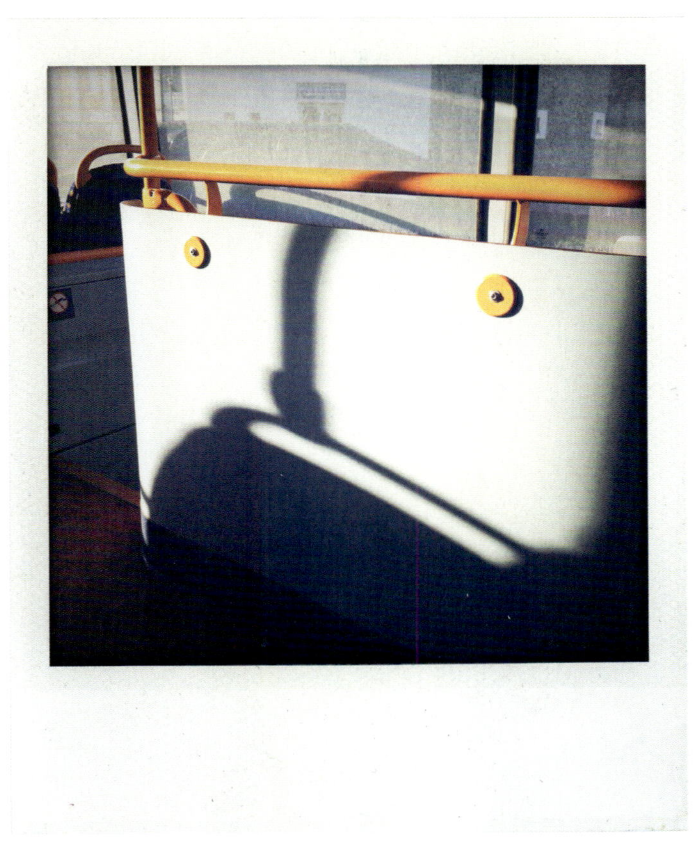

Bus shadow – Canterbury, Kent

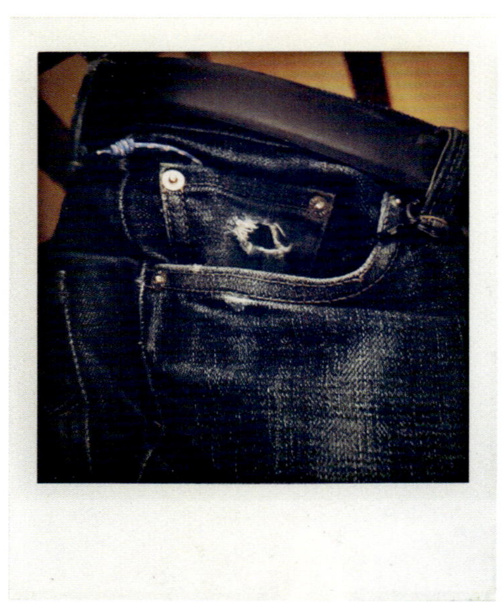

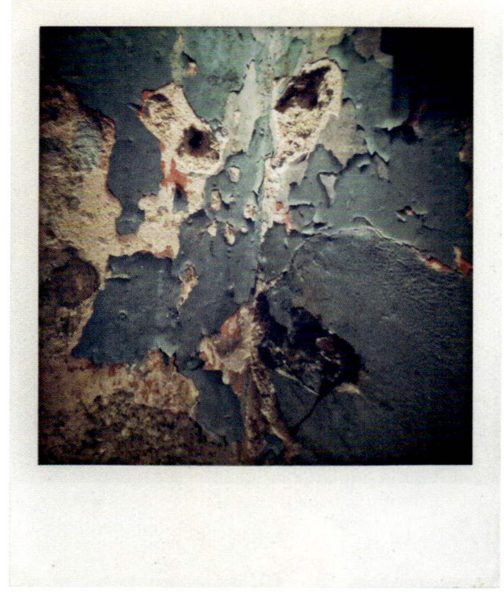

My selvedge – Home
Damaged plaster wall – Gloucester

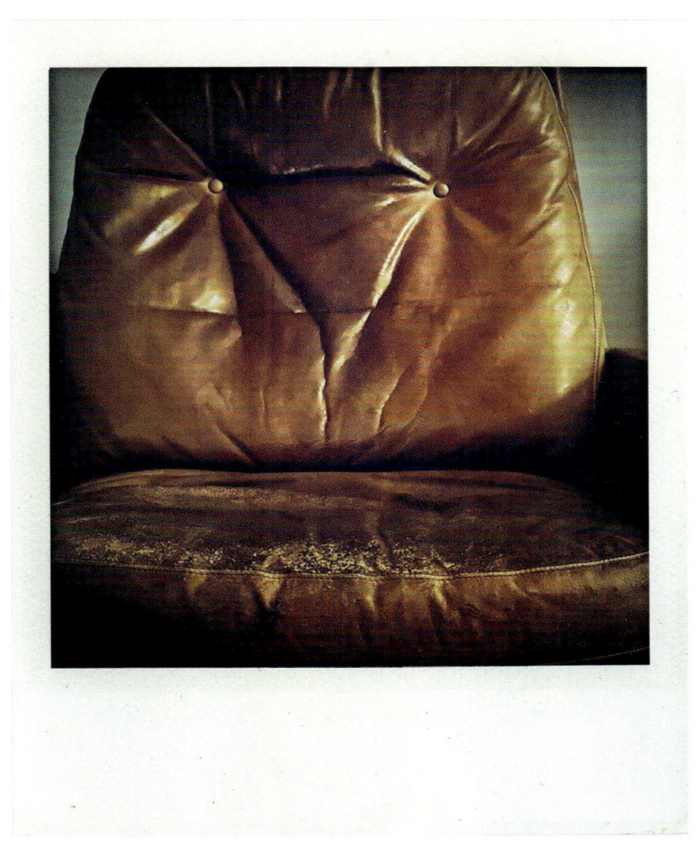

James's leather chair

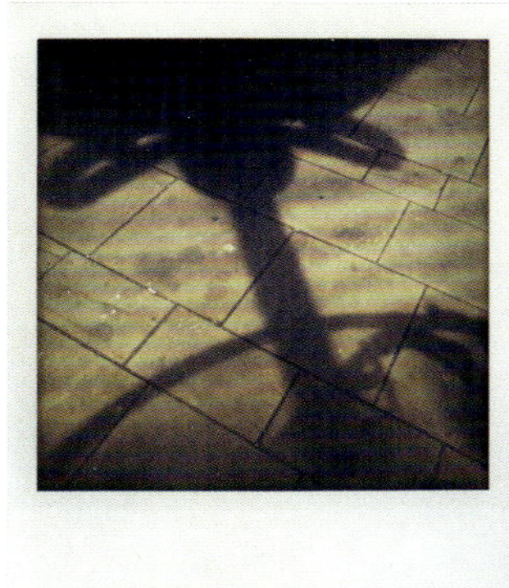 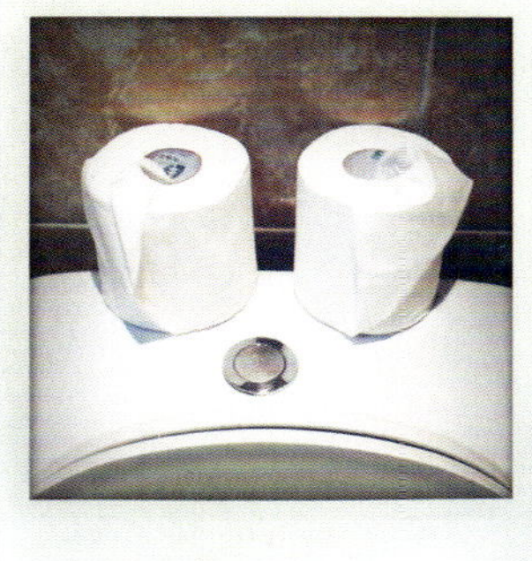 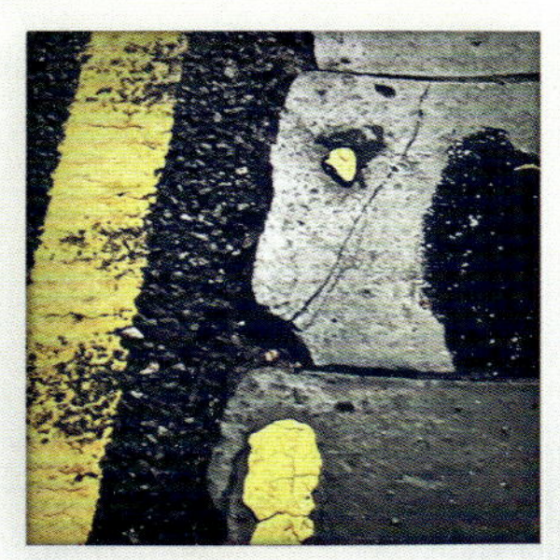

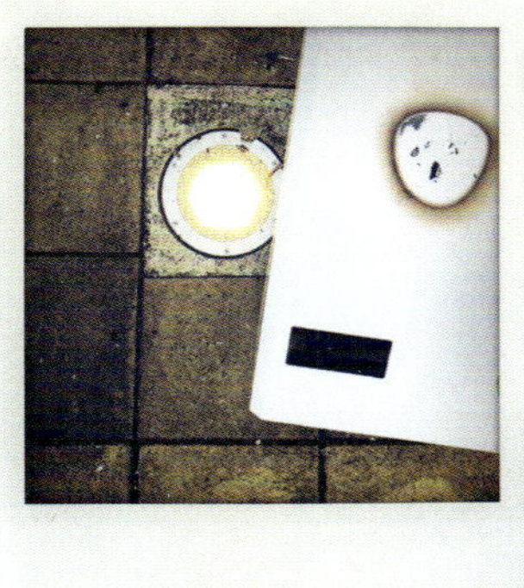 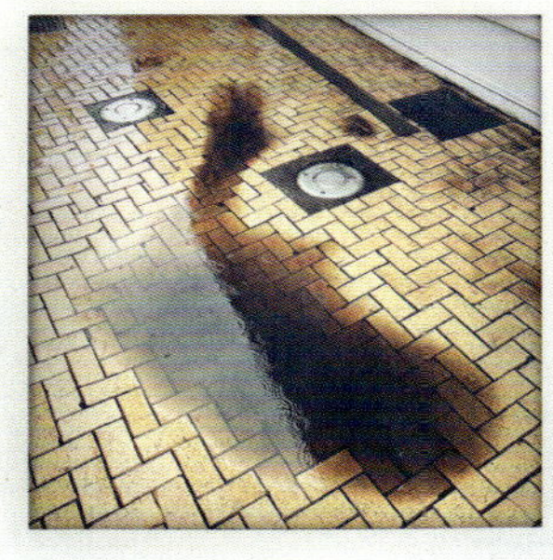 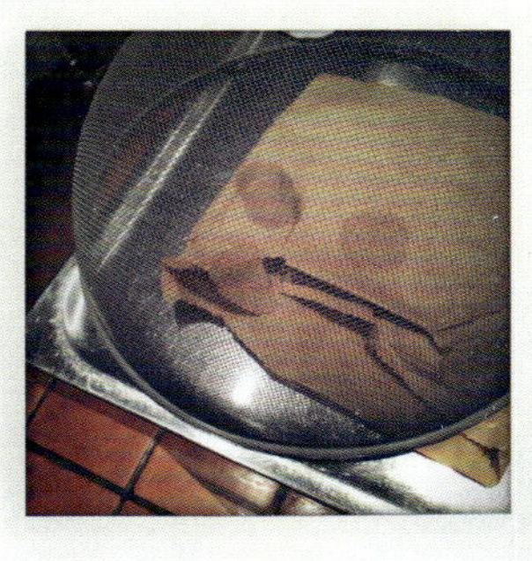

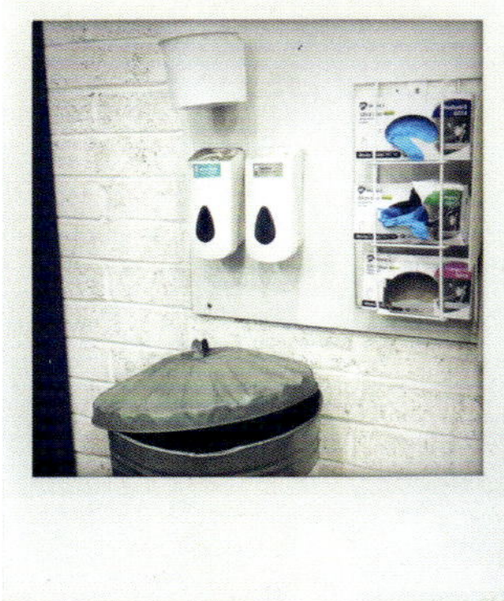 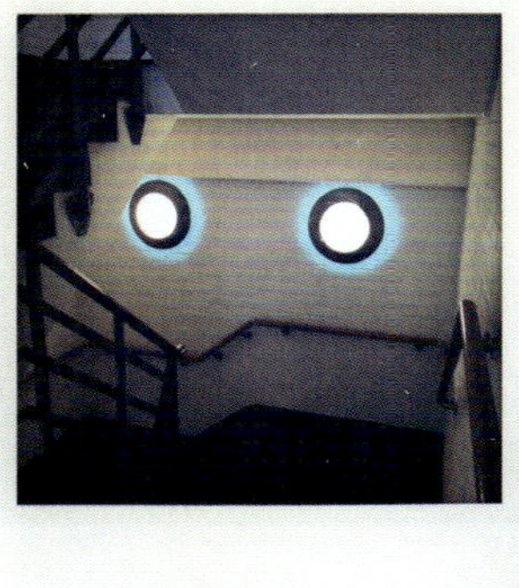 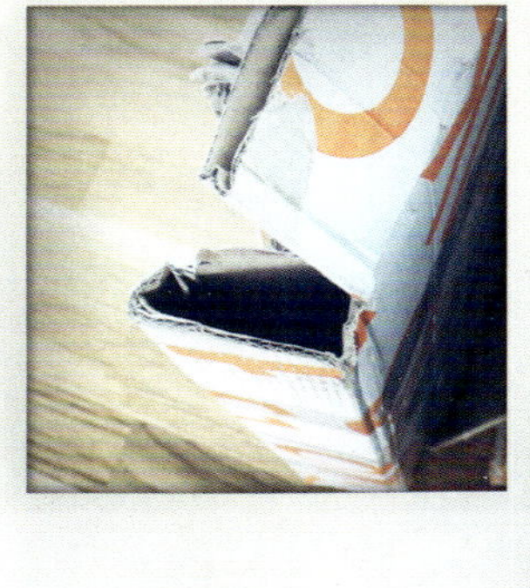

Glass table – London
Abandoned radiator – London
PPE, factory – Hampshire

Hotel – Kabul, Afghanistan
Muddy puddle – Wakefield
Office stairs – St Helers

Double yellow – London
Empty food bag – Home
Flat-pack box – Home

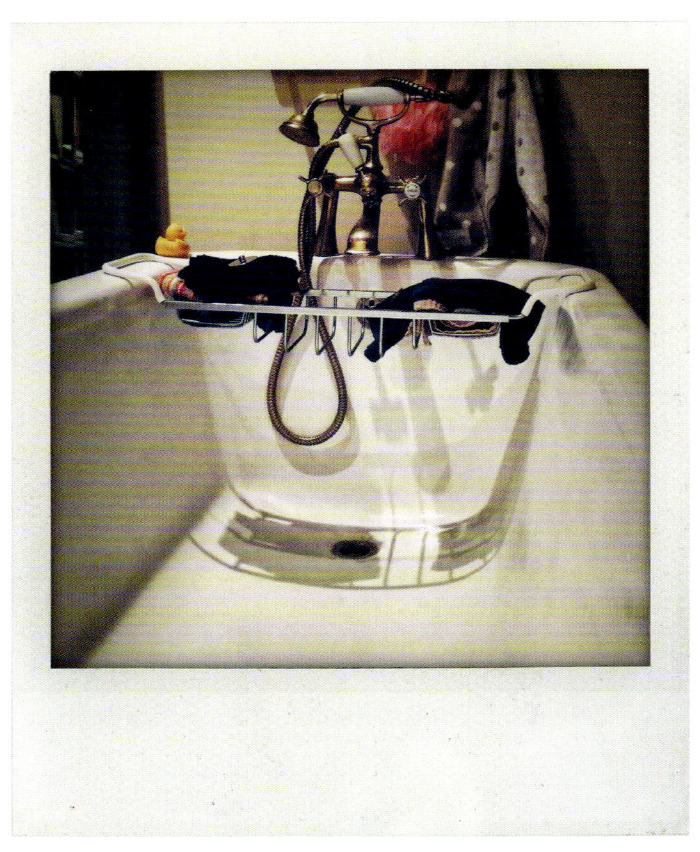

Bathroom at a friend's home

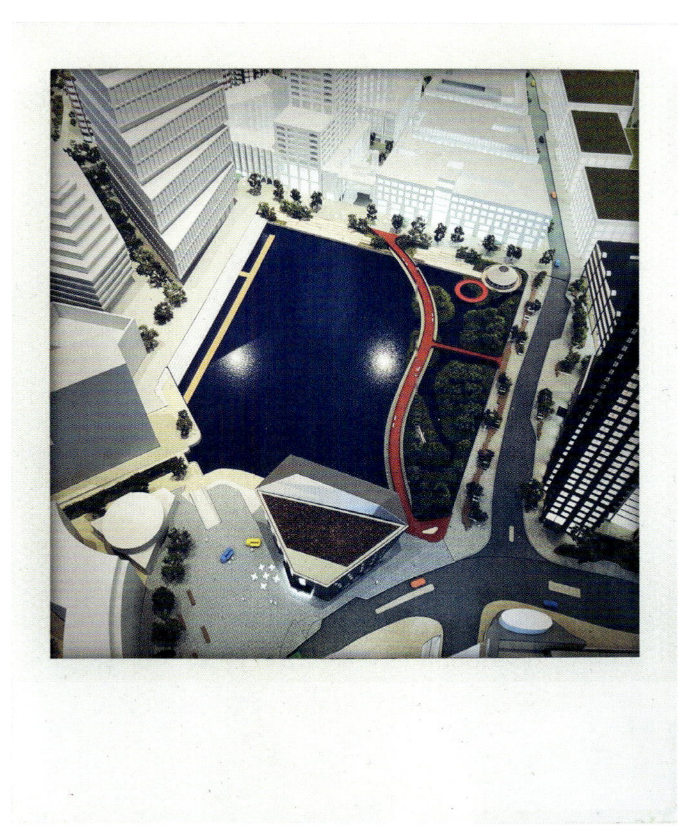

Architectural model in an office

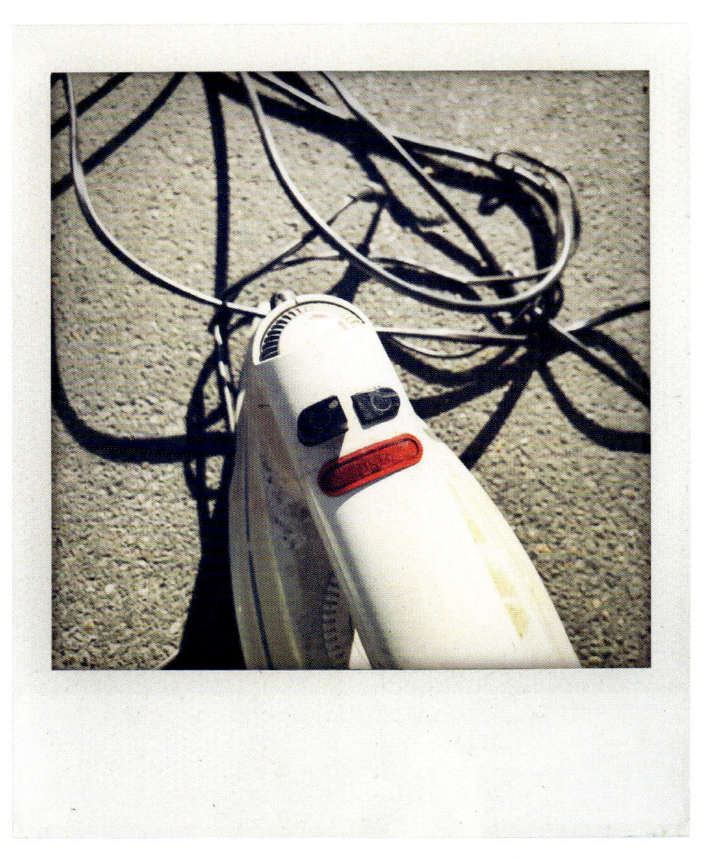

Discarded steam iron – Paris

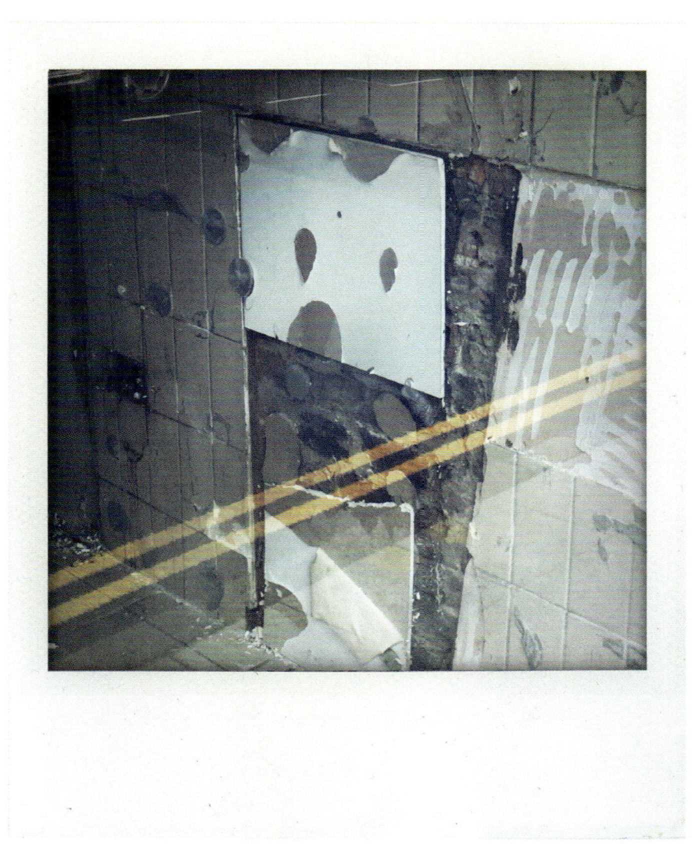

Refurb with reflections – London

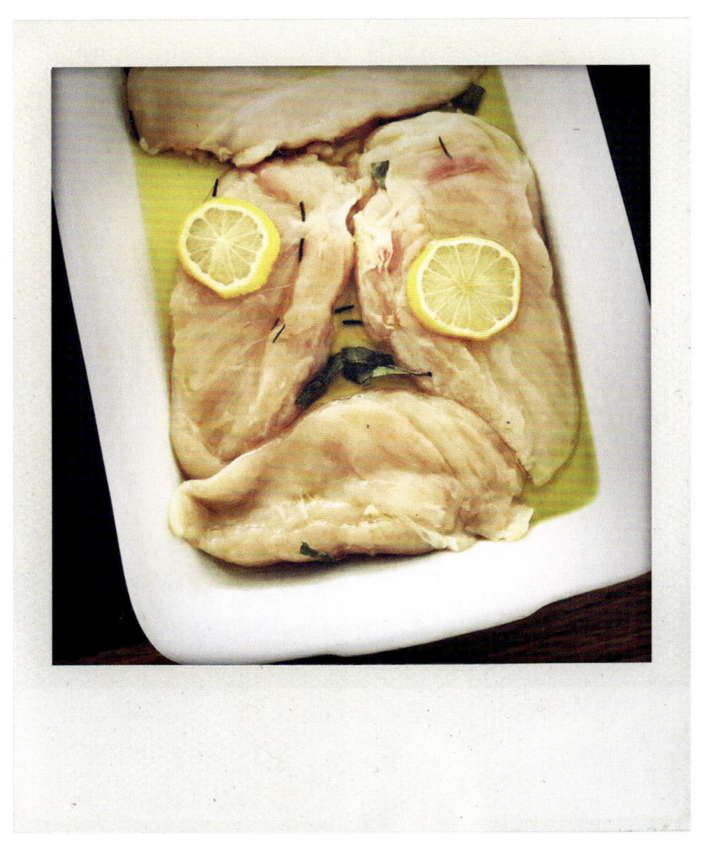

Marinating chicken – Home

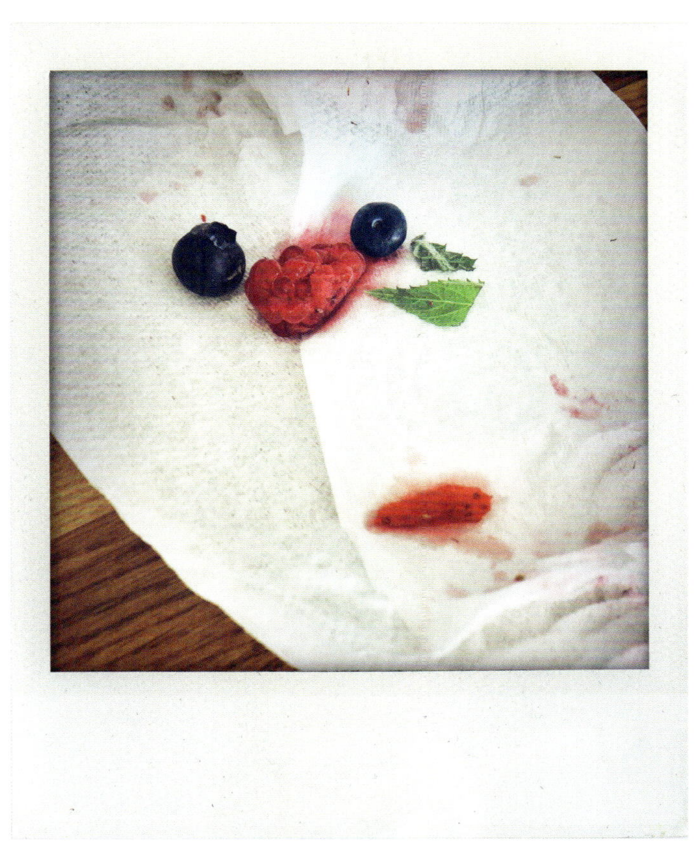

Spoiled soft fruit – Home

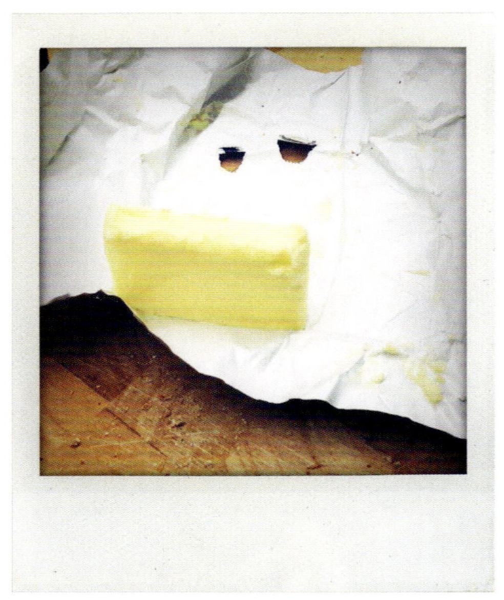

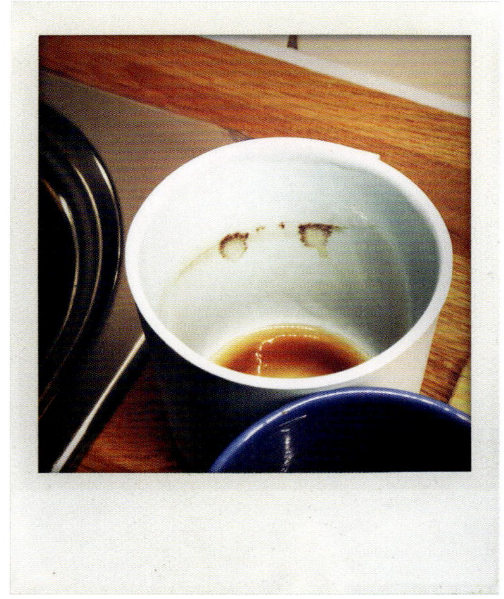

Last of the butter – Home
Coffee cup – Home

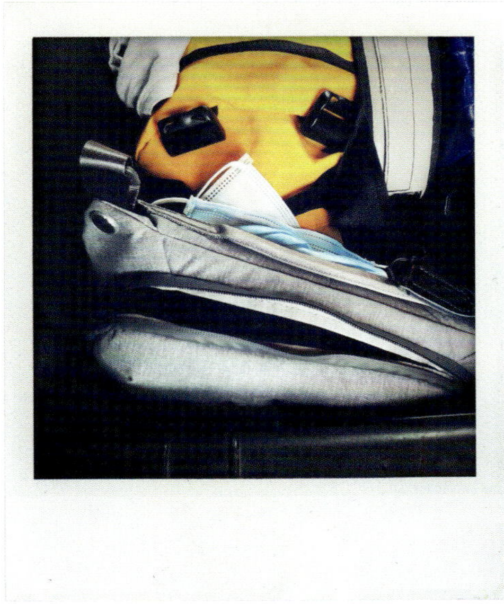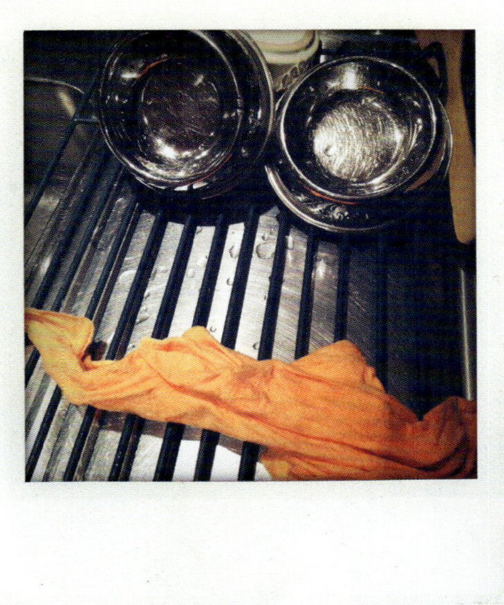

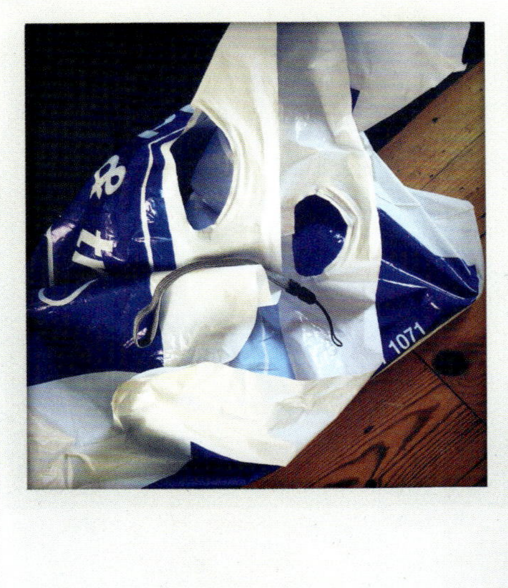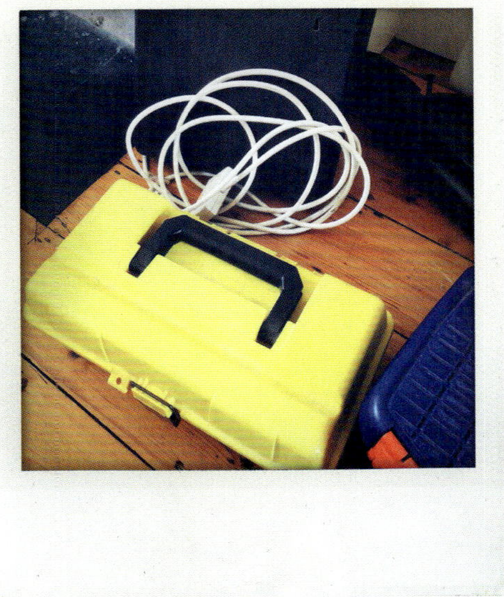

Camera bag chaos – Back seat of car
Bags ready to move house

Washing-up rack
Random objects ready to move house

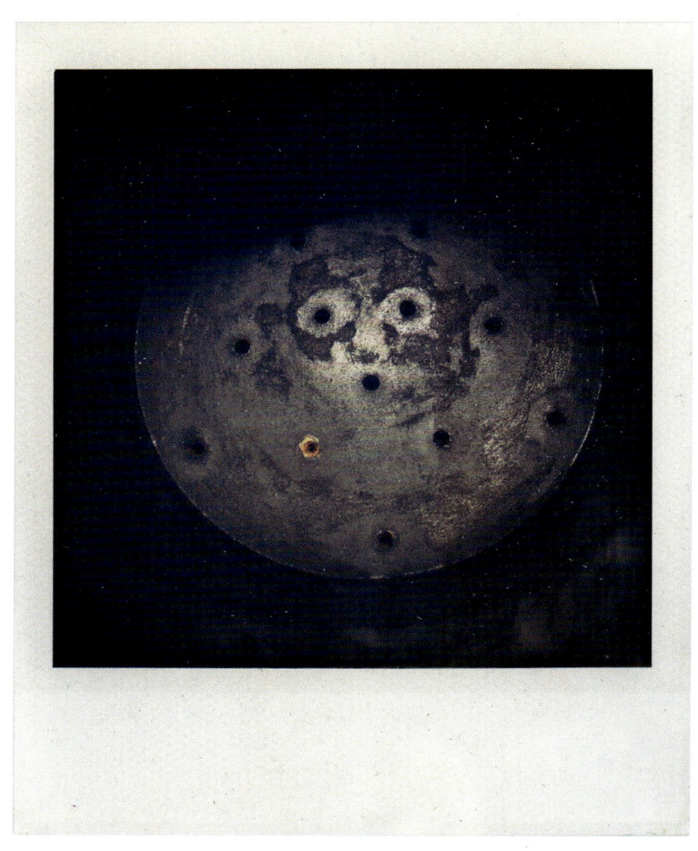

Sediment in coffee filter

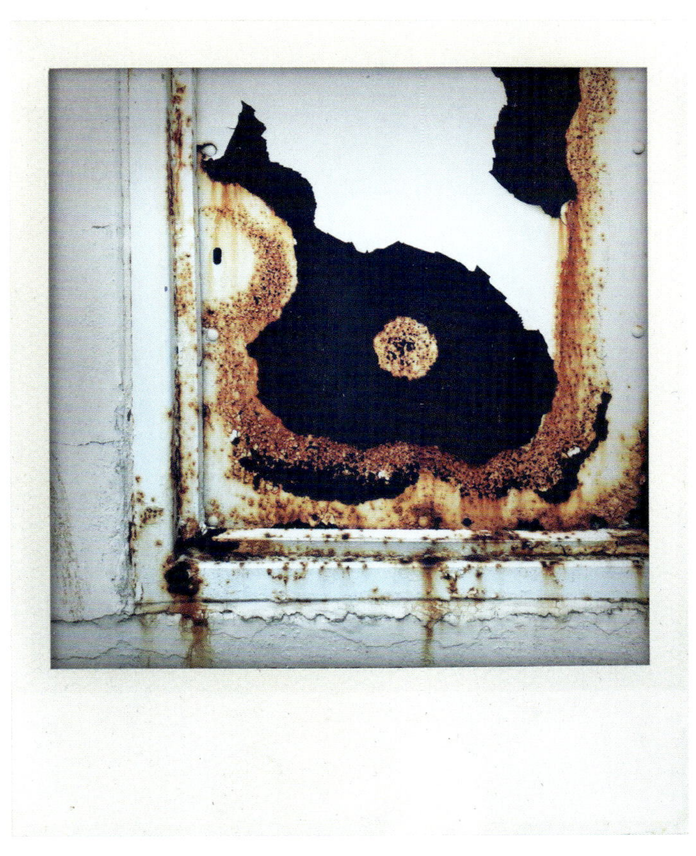

Rusting door – Folkestone, Kent

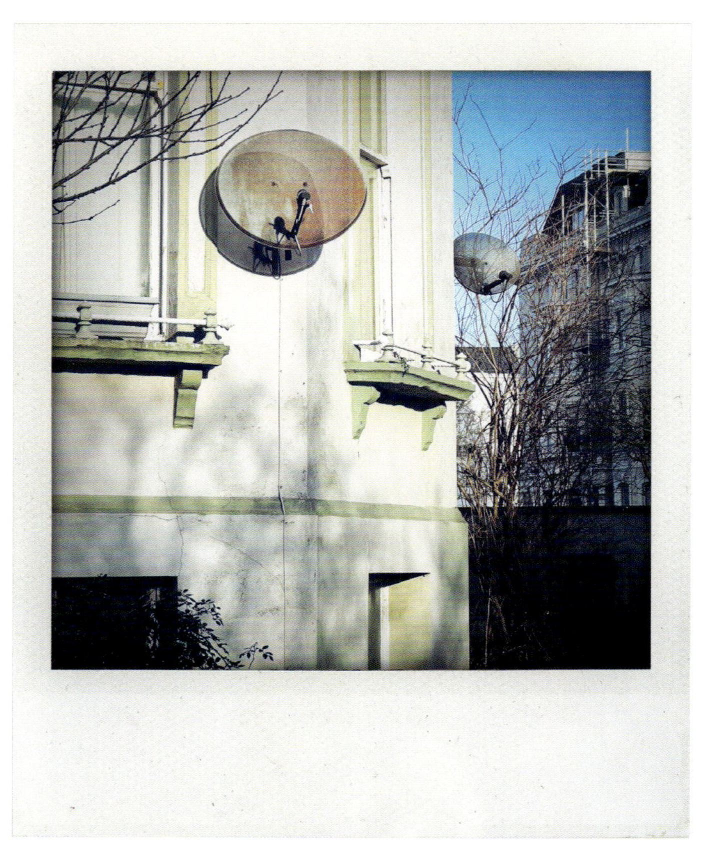

Rhodesia Hotel – Folkestone, Kent

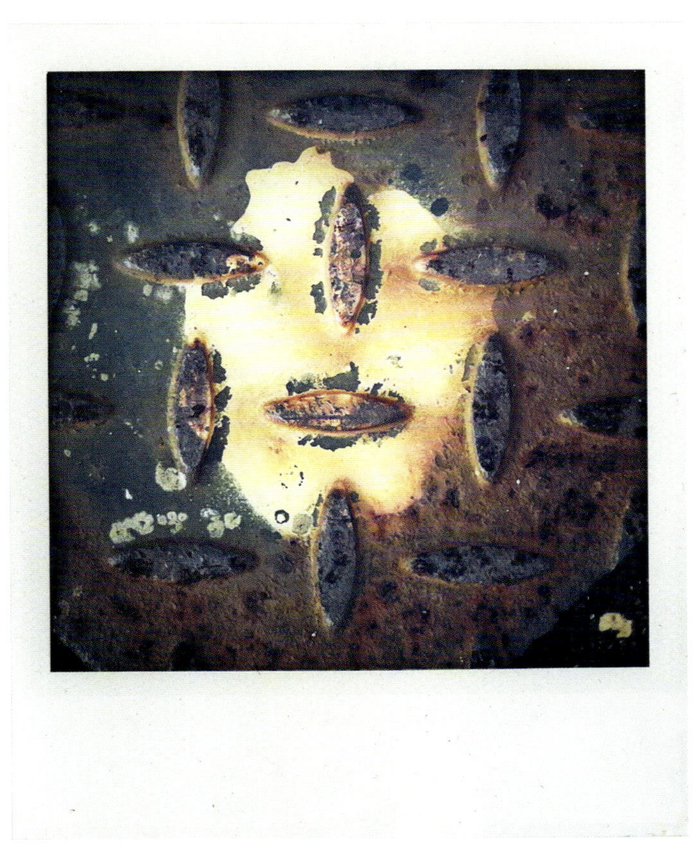

Rusting manhole cover – Cross-in-Hand, East Sussex

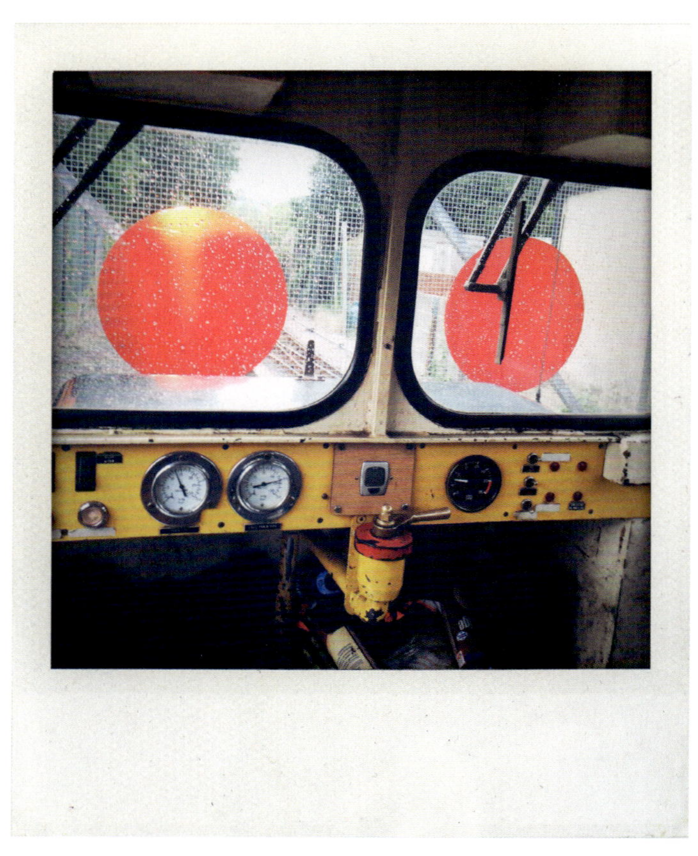

Inside the cabin of a miniature railway engine – Romney Marshes, Kent

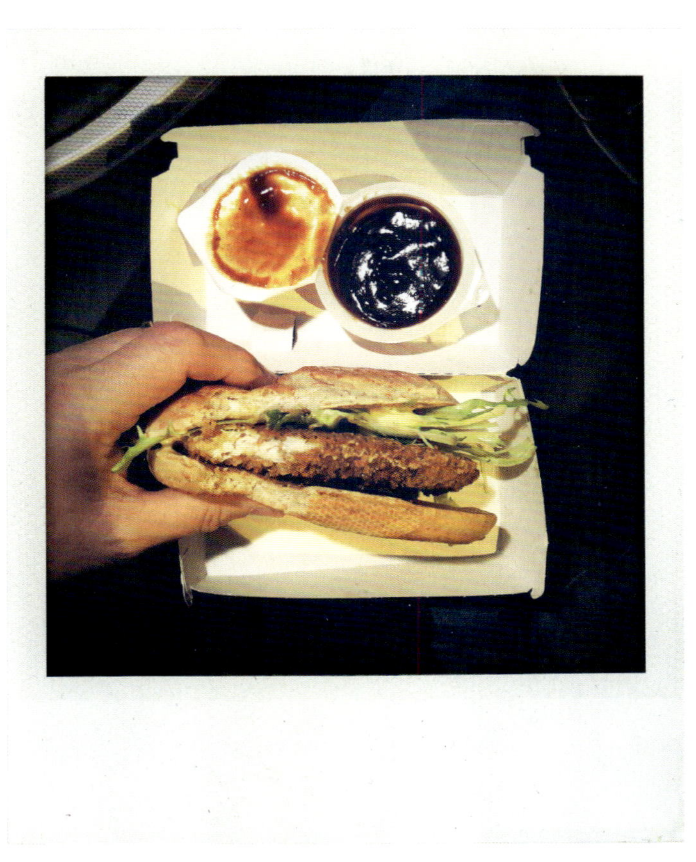

Drive-through – Hastings, East Sussex

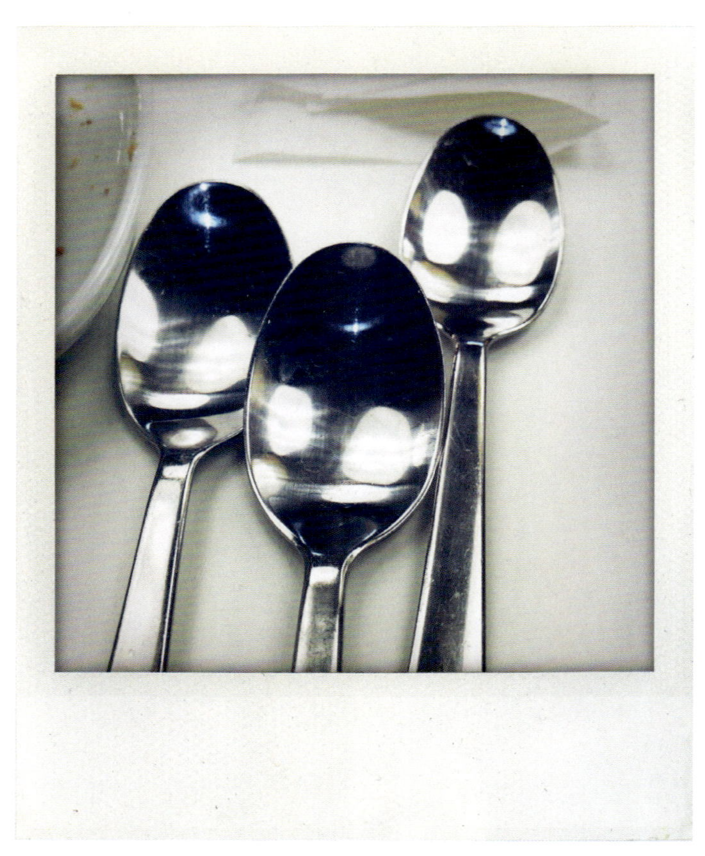

Alien teaspoons – Home

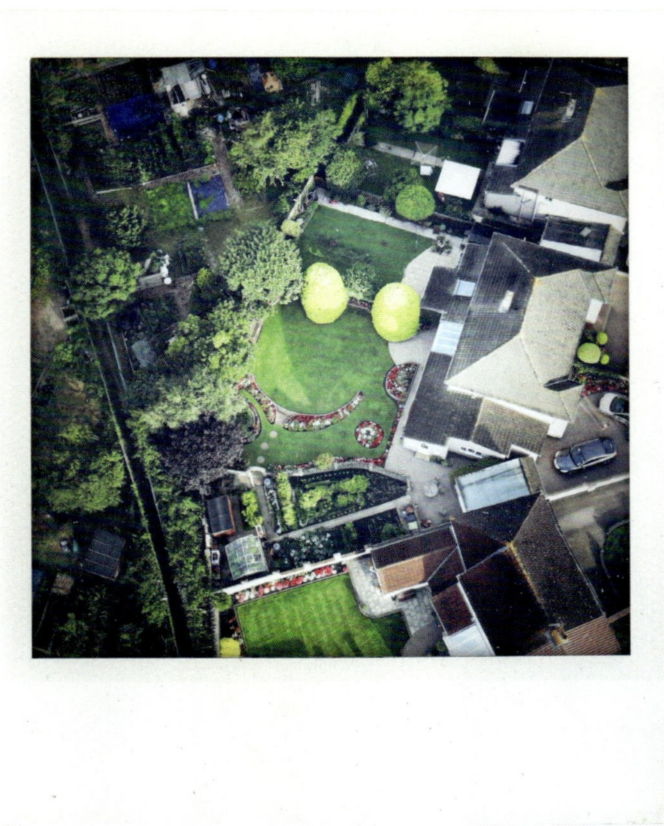

Garden seen from hot air balloon – Bristcl, Avon

Published in 2024
by Unicorn, an imprint of Unicorn Publishing Group
Charleston Studio, Meadow Business Centre
Lewes BN8 5RW
www.unicornpublishing.org

Every effort has been made to trace copyright holders and
to obtain their permission for the use of copyright material.
The publisher apologises for any errors or omissions and
would be grateful if notified of any corrections that should be
incorporated in future reprints or editions of this book.

ISBN 978-1-916846-01-2
10 9 8 7 6 5 4 3 2 1

Designed by Felicity Price-Smith
Printed by Fine Tone Ltd